Powered by

ADHD

THIS PLANNER BELONGS TO

_____

GOALS PLANNER

Start _____   *End* _____

GOALS	ACTION STEPS

ACTION REVIEW

GOALS	ACTION STEPS

ACTION REVIEW

GOALS	ACTION STEPS

ACTION REVIEW

I prefer to distinguish ADD as attention abundance
disorder. Everything is just so interesting, remarkably
at the same time.
— FRANK COPPOLA

GOALS PLANNER

Start _____   *End* _____

GOALS	ACTION STEPS

ACTION REVIEW

GOALS	ACTION STEPS

ACTION REVIEW

GOALS	ACTION STEPS

ACTION REVIEW

Nothing like ADHD and a good
fight to the death to make time fly.

−Rick Riordan

TO DO'S
Weekly

Must Do!

_____

_____

_____

Important

- _____
- _____
- _____
- _____
- _____
- _____
- _____
- _____
- _____
- _____

Less important

- _____
- _____
- _____
- _____
- _____
- _____
- _____
- _____
- _____
- _____

Notes

_____   _____

_____   _____

_____   _____

In the power of fixing the attention lies the
most precious of the intellectual habits.
— ROBERT HALL

HABIT TRACKER
Weekly

HÁBITS	MON	TUES	WED	THU	FRI	SAT	SUN
_____	◯	◯	◯	◯	◯	◯	◯
_____	◯	◯	◯	◯	◯	◯	◯
_____	◯	◯	◯	◯	◯	◯	◯
_____	◯	◯	◯	◯	◯	◯	◯
_____	◯	◯	◯	◯	◯	◯	◯
_____	◯	◯	◯	◯	◯	◯	◯
_____	◯	◯	◯	◯	◯	◯	◯
_____	◯	◯	◯	◯	◯	◯	◯
_____	◯	◯	◯	◯	◯	◯	◯
_____	◯	◯	◯	◯	◯	◯	◯
_____	◯	◯	◯	◯	◯	◯	◯
_____	◯	◯	◯	◯	◯	◯	◯
_____	◯	◯	◯	◯	◯	◯	◯
_____	◯	◯	◯	◯	◯	◯	◯

HOW DID I DO?

"I have more thoughts before breakfast
than most people have all day."
— UNKNOWN

BRAIN DUMP

Though Organizer

MUST DO	SHOULD DO

COULD START	MUST DO

DAILY PLANNER

TODAY'S GOALS

MOOD:

WATER INTAKE:

THINGS TO GET DONE TODAY:

_____
_____
_____
_____
_____
_____
_____
_____

TODAY'S APPOINTMENT:

TIME:	EVENT:

PRIORITIES WITH CONSEQUENCES

A
A
A

FOR TOMORROW:

_____
_____
_____
_____
_____

		1	2	3	4	5	6	7	8	9	10
IMPULSIVITY	Easily Frustrated	1	2	3	4	5	6	7	8	9	10
	Acting Without Thikining	1	2	3	4	5	6	7	8	9	10
	Interrupting Others	1	2	3	4	5	6	7	8	9	10
	Emotional Outbursts	1	2	3	4	5	6	7	8	9	10
HYPERACTIVITY	Difficulty Sleeping	1	2	3	4	5	6	7	8	9	10
	Constantly Moving	1	2	3	4	5	6	7	8	9	10
	Unable to Sit Still / Fidgeting	1	2	3	4	5	6	7	8	9	10
	Excessive Talking	1	2	3	4	5	6	7	8	9	10
INATTENTION	Easily Distracted	1	2	3	4	5	6	7	8	9	10
	Careless Mistakes	1	2	3	4	5	6	7	8	9	10
	Short Attention	1	2	3	4	5	6	7	8	9	10
	Forgetfulness	1	2	3	4	5	6	7	8	9	10

Date _____

DAILY PLANNER

Today's Goals

Mood:
😄 🙂 😐 🙁 😢

Water Intake:
◇ ◇ ◇ ◇ ◇ ◇ ◇ ◇

Priorities with Consequences
A⁺
A⁺
A⁺

Things to get done today:
_____
_____
_____
_____
_____
_____
_____

Today's appointment:

TIME:	EVENT:

For tomorrow:
_____
_____
_____
_____
_____

		1	2	3	4	5	6	7	8	9	10
IMPULSIVITY	Easily Frustrated	1	2	3	4	5	6	7	8	9	10
	Acting Without Thikining	1	2	3	4	5	6	7	8	9	10
	Interrupting Others	1	2	3	4	5	6	7	8	9	10
	Emotional Outbursts	1	2	3	4	5	6	7	8	9	10
HYPERACTIVITY	Difficulty Sleeping	1	2	3	4	5	6	7	8	9	10
	Constantly Moving	1	2	3	4	5	6	7	8	9	10
	Unable to Sit Still / Fidgeting	1	2	3	4	5	6	7	8	9	10
	Excessive Talking	1	2	3	4	5	6	7	8	9	10
INATTENTION	Easily Distracted	1	2	3	4	5	6	7	8	9	10
	Careless Mistakes	1	2	3	4	5	6	7	8	9	10
	Short Attention	1	2	3	4	5	6	7	8	9	10
	Forgetfulness	1	2	3	4	5	6	7	8	9	10

DAILY PLANNER

TODAY'S GOALS

MOOD:

PRIORITIES WITH CONSEQUENCES

A⁺

WATER INTAKE:

A⁺

THINGS TO GET DONE TODAY:

TODAY'S APPOINTMENT:

A⁺

TIME: EVENT:

FOR TOMORROW:

		1	2	3	4	5	6	7	8	9	10
IMPULSIVITY	Easily Frustrated	1	2	3	4	5	6	7	8	9	10
	Acting Without Thikining	1	2	3	4	5	6	7	8	9	10
	Interrupting Others	1	2	3	4	5	6	7	8	9	10
	Emotional Outbursts	1	2	3	4	5	6	7	8	9	10
HYPERACTIVITY	Difficulty Sleeping	1	2	3	4	5	6	7	8	9	10
	Constantly Moving	1	2	3	4	5	6	7	8	9	10
	Unable to Sit Still / Fidgeting	1	2	3	4	5	6	7	8	9	10
	Excessive Talking	1	2	3	4	5	6	7	8	9	10
INATTENTION	Easily Distracted	1	2	3	4	5	6	7	8	9	10
	Careless Mistakes	1	2	3	4	5	6	7	8	9	10
	Short Attention	1	2	3	4	5	6	7	8	9	10
	Forgetfulness	1	2	3	4	5	6	7	8	9	10

Date _____

DAILY PLANNER

Today's goals

Mood:

😄 🙂 😐 ☹️ 😖

Water Intake:

💧 💧 💧 💧 💧 💧 💧 💧

Priorities with Consequences

Things to get done today:

_____
_____
_____
_____
_____
_____
_____
_____

Today's appointment:

Time:	Event:

For tomorrow:

_____
_____
_____
_____

		1	2	3	4	5	6	7	8	9	10
IMPULSIVITY	Easily Frustrated	1	2	3	4	5	6	7	8	9	10
	Acting Without Thikining	1	2	3	4	5	6	7	8	9	10
	Interrupting Others	1	2	3	4	5	6	7	8	9	10
	Emotional Outbursts	1	2	3	4	5	6	7	8	9	10
HYPERACTIVITY	Difficulty Sleeping	1	2	3	4	5	6	7	8	9	10
	Constantly Moving	1	2	3	4	5	6	7	8	9	10
	Unable to Sit Still / Fidgeting	1	2	3	4	5	6	7	8	9	10
	Excessive Talking	1	2	3	4	5	6	7	8	9	10
INATTENTION	Easily Distracted	1	2	3	4	5	6	7	8	9	10
	Careless Mistakes	1	2	3	4	5	6	7	8	9	10
	Short Attention	1	2	3	4	5	6	7	8	9	10
	Forgetfulness	1	2	3	4	5	6	7	8	9	10

$\mathcal{Date}$ _____

DAILY PLANNER

🎯 Today's goals

Mood:
😊 🙂 😐 🙁 ☹️

Water Intake:
💧💧💧💧💧💧💧💧

Priorities with Consequences

[A]

[A]

[A]

Things to get done today:
_____
_____
_____
_____
_____
_____
_____
_____
_____

Today's appointment:

Time:	Event:

For tomorrow:
_____
_____
_____
_____
_____

		1	2	3	4	5	6	7	8	9	10
IMPULSIVITY	Easily Frustrated	1	2	3	4	5	6	7	8	9	10
	Acting Without Thikining	1	2	3	4	5	6	7	8	9	10
	Interrupting Others	1	2	3	4	5	6	7	8	9	10
	Emotional Outbursts	1	2	3	4	5	6	7	8	9	10
HYPERACTIVITY	Difficulty Sleeping	1	2	3	4	5	6	7	8	9	10
	Constantly Moving	1	2	3	4	5	6	7	8	9	10
	Unable to Sit Still / Fidgeting	1	2	3	4	5	6	7	8	9	10
	Excessive Talking	1	2	3	4	5	6	7	8	9	10
INATTENTION	Easily Distracted	1	2	3	4	5	6	7	8	9	10
	Careless Mistakes	1	2	3	4	5	6	7	8	9	10
	Short Attention	1	2	3	4	5	6	7	8	9	10
	Forgetfulness	1	2	3	4	5	6	7	8	9	10

Date _____

DAILY PLANNER

Today's Goals

Mood:

😊 🙂 😐 🙁 😢

Water Intake:

💧💧💧💧💧💧💧💧

Priorities with Consequences

A⁺

A⁺

A⁺

Things to get done today:

_____
_____
_____
_____
_____
_____
_____

Today's appointment:

TIME: EVENT:

For tomorrow:

_____
_____
_____
_____
_____

		1	2	3	4	5	6	7	8	9	10
IMPULSIVITY	Easily Frustrated	1	2	3	4	5	6	7	8	9	10
	Acting Without Thikining	1	2	3	4	5	6	7	8	9	10
	Interrupting Others	1	2	3	4	5	6	7	8	9	10
	Emotional Outbursts	1	2	3	4	5	6	7	8	9	10
HYPERACTIVITY	Difficulty Sleeping	1	2	3	4	5	6	7	8	9	10
	Constantly Moving	1	2	3	4	5	6	7	8	9	10
	Unable to Sit Still / Fidgeting	1	2	3	4	5	6	7	8	9	10
	Excessive Talking	1	2	3	4	5	6	7	8	9	10
INATTENTION	Easily Distracted	1	2	3	4	5	6	7	8	9	10
	Careless Mistakes	1	2	3	4	5	6	7	8	9	10
	Short Attention	1	2	3	4	5	6	7	8	9	10
	Forgetfulness	1	2	3	4	5	6	7	8	9	10

DAILY PLANNER

TODAY'S GOALS

MOOD:

😄 🙂 😐 🙁 ☹️

WATER INTAKE:

💧💧💧💧💧💧💧💧💧

PRIORITIES WITH CONSEQUENCES

A⁺

A⁺

A⁺

THINGS TO GET DONE TODAY:

_____
_____
_____
_____
_____
_____
_____

TODAY'S APPOINTMENT:

TIME:	EVENT:

FOR TOMORROW:

_____
_____
_____
_____
_____

		1	2	3	4	5	6	7	8	9	10
IMPULSIVITY	Easily Frustrated	1	2	3	4	5	6	7	8	9	10
	Acting Without Thikining	1	2	3	4	5	6	7	8	9	10
	Interrupting Others	1	2	3	4	5	6	7	8	9	10
	Emotional Outbursts	1	2	3	4	5	6	7	8	9	10
HYPERACTIVITY	Difficulty Sleeping	1	2	3	4	5	6	7	8	9	10
	Constantly Moving	1	2	3	4	5	6	7	8	9	10
	Unable to Sit Still / Fidgeting	1	2	3	4	5	6	7	8	9	10
	Excessive Talking	1	2	3	4	5	6	7	8	9	10
INATTENTION	Easily Distracted	1	2	3	4	5	6	7	8	9	10
	Careless Mistakes	1	2	3	4	5	6	7	8	9	10
	Short Attention	1	2	3	4	5	6	7	8	9	10
	Forgetfulness	1	2	3	4	5	6	7	8	9	10

MEDICATION
Tracker

	MEDICATION	DOSAGE	FREQUENCY	TAKEN
MONDAY				
TUESDAY				
WEDNESDAY				
THURSDAY				
FRIDAY				
SATURDAY				
SUNDAY				

NOTES

Nothing like ADHD and a good
fight to the death to make time fly.

—Rick Riordan

TO DO'S
Weekly

Must Do!

_____

_____

_____

Important

- _____
- _____
- _____
- _____
- _____
- _____
- _____
- _____
- _____
- _____

Less important

- _____
- _____
- _____
- _____
- _____
- _____
- _____
- _____
- _____
- _____

Notes

_____   _____

_____   _____

_____   _____

_____   _____

In the power of fixing the attention lies the
most precious of the intellectual habits.
– ROBERT HALL

HABIT TRACKER
Weekly

HÁBITS	MON	TUES	WED	THU	FRI	SAT	SUN
	○	○	○	○	○	○	○
	○	○	○	○	○	○	○
	○	○	○	○	○	○	○
	○	○	○	○	○	○	○
	○	○	○	○	○	○	○
	○	○	○	○	○	○	○
	○	○	○	○	○	○	○
	○	○	○	○	○	○	○
	○	○	○	○	○	○	○
	○	○	○	○	○	○	○
	○	○	○	○	○	○	○
	○	○	○	○	○	○	○
	○	○	○	○	○	○	○
	○	○	○	○	○	○	○

HOW DID I DO?

"I have more thoughts before breakfast
than most people have all day."
— UNKNOWN

BRAIN DUMP

Though Organizer

MUST DO	SHOULD DO
COULD START	MUST DO

DAILY PLANNER

TODAY'S GOALS

MOOD:

😄 🙂 😐 🙁 😣

WATER INTAKE:

⬡ ⬡ ⬡ ⬡ ⬡ ⬡ ⬡ ⬡

PRIORITIES WITH CONSEQUENCES

A⁺

A⁺

A⁺

THINGS TO GET DONE TODAY:

_____
_____
_____
_____
_____
_____
_____
_____

TODAY'S APPOINTMENT:

TIME:	EVENT:

FOR TOMORROW:

_____
_____
_____
_____
_____

		1	2	3	4	5	6	7	8	9	10
IMPULSIVITY	Easily Frustrated	1	2	3	4	5	6	7	8	9	10
	Acting Without Thikining	1	2	3	4	5	6	7	8	9	10
	Interrupting Others	1	2	3	4	5	6	7	8	9	10
	Emotional Outbursts	1	2	3	4	5	6	7	8	9	10
HYPERACTIVITY	Difficulty Sleeping	1	2	3	4	5	6	7	8	9	10
	Constantly Moving	1	2	3	4	5	6	7	8	9	10
	Unable to Sit Still / Fidgeting	1	2	3	4	5	6	7	8	9	10
	Excessive Talking	1	2	3	4	5	6	7	8	9	10
INATTENTION	Easily Distracted	1	2	3	4	5	6	7	8	9	10
	Careless Mistakes	1	2	3	4	5	6	7	8	9	10
	Short Attention	1	2	3	4	5	6	7	8	9	10
	Forgetfulness	1	2	3	4	5	6	7	8	9	10

Date _____

DAILY PLANNER

Today's goals

Mood:

😄 🙂 😐 🙁 😢

Water Intake:

💧💧💧💧💧💧💧💧

Priorities with Consequences

A⁺

A⁺

A⁺

Things to get done today:

_____
_____
_____
_____
_____
_____
_____
_____

Today's appointment:

TIME: EVENT:

_____
_____
_____
_____
_____
_____

For tomorrow:

_____
_____
_____
_____
_____

		1	2	3	4	5	6	7	8	9	10
IMPULSIVITY	Easily Frustrated	1	2	3	4	5	6	7	8	9	10
	Acting Without Thikining	1	2	3	4	5	6	7	8	9	10
	Interrupting Others	1	2	3	4	5	6	7	8	9	10
	Emotional Outbursts	1	2	3	4	5	6	7	8	9	10
HYPERACTIVITY	Difficulty Sleeping	1	2	3	4	5	6	7	8	9	10
	Constantly Moving	1	2	3	4	5	6	7	8	9	10
	Unable to Sit Still / Fidgeting	1	2	3	4	5	6	7	8	9	10
	Excessive Talking	1	2	3	4	5	6	7	8	9	10
INATTENTION	Easily Distracted	1	2	3	4	5	6	7	8	9	10
	Careless Mistakes	1	2	3	4	5	6	7	8	9	10
	Short Attention	1	2	3	4	5	6	7	8	9	10
	Forgetfulness	1	2	3	4	5	6	7	8	9	10

Date _____

DAILY PLANNER

TODAY'S GOALS

MOOD:

WATER INTAKE:

PRIORITIES WITH CONSEQUENCES

A⁺

A⁺

A⁺

THINGS TO GET DONE TODAY:

_____
_____
_____
_____
_____
_____
_____
_____

TODAY'S APPOINTMENT:

TIME:	EVENT:

FOR TOMORROW:

_____
_____
_____
_____
_____
_____

		1	2	3	4	5	6	7	8	9	10
IMPULSIVITY	Easily Frustrated	1	2	3	4	5	6	7	8	9	10
	Acting Without Thikining	1	2	3	4	5	6	7	8	9	10
	Interrupting Others	1	2	3	4	5	6	7	8	9	10
	Emotional Outbursts	1	2	3	4	5	6	7	8	9	10
HYPERACTIVITY	Difficulty Sleeping	1	2	3	4	5	6	7	8	9	10
	Constantly Moving	1	2	3	4	5	6	7	8	9	10
	Unable to Sit Still / Fidgeting	1	2	3	4	5	6	7	8	9	10
	Excessive Talking	1	2	3	4	5	6	7	8	9	10
INATTENTION	Easily Distracted	1	2	3	4	5	6	7	8	9	10
	Careless Mistakes	1	2	3	4	5	6	7	8	9	10
	Short Attention	1	2	3	4	5	6	7	8	9	10
	Forgetfulness	1	2	3	4	5	6	7	8	9	10

Date _____

DAILY PLANNER

Today's goals

Mood:

Water Intake:

Priorities with Consequences

Things to get done today:
_____
_____
_____
_____
_____
_____
_____

Today's appointment:

TIME:	EVENT:

For tomorrow:
_____
_____
_____
_____

		1	2	3	4	5	6	7	8	9	10
IMPULSIVITY	Easily Frustrated	1	2	3	4	5	6	7	8	9	10
	Acting Without Thikining	1	2	3	4	5	6	7	8	9	10
	Interrupting Others	1	2	3	4	5	6	7	8	9	10
	Emotional Outbursts	1	2	3	4	5	6	7	8	9	10
HYPERACTIVITY	Difficulty Sleeping	1	2	3	4	5	6	7	8	9	10
	Constantly Moving	1	2	3	4	5	6	7	8	9	10
	Unable to Sit Still / Fidgeting	1	2	3	4	5	6	7	8	9	10
	Excessive Talking	1	2	3	4	5	6	7	8	9	10
INATTENTION	Easily Distracted	1	2	3	4	5	6	7	8	9	10
	Careless Mistakes	1	2	3	4	5	6	7	8	9	10
	Short Attention	1	2	3	4	5	6	7	8	9	10
	Forgetfulness	1	2	3	4	5	6	7	8	9	10

Date _____

DAILY PLANNER

Today's goals

Mood:

Priorities with Consequences

A⁺

Water Intake:

A⁺

Things to get done today:

_____
_____
_____
_____
_____
_____
_____
_____

Today's appointment:

TIME: EVENT:

A⁺

For tomorrow:

_____
_____
_____
_____
_____

		1	2	3	4	5	6	7	8	9	10
IMPULSIVITY	Easily Frustrated	1	2	3	4	5	6	7	8	9	10
	Acting Without Thikining	1	2	3	4	5	6	7	8	9	10
	Interrupting Others	1	2	3	4	5	6	7	8	9	10
	Emotional Outbursts	1	2	3	4	5	6	7	8	9	10
HYPERACTIVITY	Difficulty Sleeping	1	2	3	4	5	6	7	8	9	10
	Constantly Moving	1	2	3	4	5	6	7	8	9	10
	Unable to Sit Still / Fidgeting	1	2	3	4	5	6	7	8	9	10
	Excessive Talking	1	2	3	4	5	6	7	8	9	10
INATTENTION	Easily Distracted	1	2	3	4	5	6	7	8	9	10
	Careless Mistakes	1	2	3	4	5	6	7	8	9	10
	Short Attention	1	2	3	4	5	6	7	8	9	10
	Forgetfulness	1	2	3	4	5	6	7	8	9	10

 *Date* _____

DAILY PLANNER

🎯 TODAY'S GOALS

MOOD:

😄 🙂 😐 🙁 😢

WATER INTAKE:

💧 💧 💧 💧 💧 💧 💧

PRIORITIES WITH CONSEQUENCES

A⁺

A⁺

A⁺

THINGS TO GET DONE TODAY:

_____
_____
_____
_____
_____
_____
_____
_____

TODAY'S APPOINTMENT:

TIME:	EVENT:

FOR TOMORROW:

_____
_____
_____
_____
_____

		1	2	3	4	5	6	7	8	9	10
IMPULSIVITY	Easily Frustrated	1	2	3	4	5	6	7	8	9	10
	Acting Without Thikining	1	2	3	4	5	6	7	8	9	10
	Interrupting Others	1	2	3	4	5	6	7	8	9	10
	Emotional Outbursts	1	2	3	4	5	6	7	8	9	10
HYPERACTIVITY	Difficulty Sleeping	1	2	3	4	5	6	7	8	9	10
	Constantly Moving	1	2	3	4	5	6	7	8	9	10
	Unable to Sit Still / Fidgeting	1	2	3	4	5	6	7	8	9	10
	Excessive Talking	1	2	3	4	5	6	7	8	9	10
INATTENTION	Easily Distracted	1	2	3	4	5	6	7	8	9	10
	Careless Mistakes	1	2	3	4	5	6	7	8	9	10
	Short Attention	1	2	3	4	5	6	7	8	9	10
	Forgetfulness	1	2	3	4	5	6	7	8	9	10

 Date _____

DAILY PLANNER

Today's goals

Mood:

Water Intake:

Priorities with Consequences

A⁺

A⁺

A⁺

Things to get done today:

_____
_____
_____
_____
_____
_____
_____
_____
_____
_____

Today's appointment:

TIME: | EVENT:
_____ | _____
_____ | _____
_____ | _____
_____ | _____
_____ | _____
_____ | _____
_____ | _____
_____ | _____

For tomorrow:

_____
_____
_____
_____
_____
_____

		1	2	3	4	5	6	7	8	9	10
IMPULSIVITY	Easily Frustrated	1	2	3	4	5	6	7	8	9	10
	Acting Without Thikining	1	2	3	4	5	6	7	8	9	10
	Interrupting Others	1	2	3	4	5	6	7	8	9	10
	Emotional Outbursts	1	2	3	4	5	6	7	8	9	10
HYPERACTIVITY	Difficulty Sleeping	1	2	3	4	5	6	7	8	9	10
	Constantly Moving	1	2	3	4	5	6	7	8	9	10
	Unable to Sit Still / Fidgeting	1	2	3	4	5	6	7	8	9	10
	Excessive Talking	1	2	3	4	5	6	7	8	9	10
INATTENTION	Easily Distracted	1	2	3	4	5	6	7	8	9	10
	Careless Mistakes	1	2	3	4	5	6	7	8	9	10
	Short Attention	1	2	3	4	5	6	7	8	9	10
	Forgetfulness	1	2	3	4	5	6	7	8	9	10

> "It's like being a cat with 100 people with laser pointers."
> — JAMIE HYNDS

MEDICATION
Tracker

	MEDICATION	DOSAGE	FREQUENCY	TAKEN
MONDAY				
TUESDAY				
WEDNESDAY				
THURSDAY				
FRIDAY				
SATURDAY				
SUNDAY				

NOTES

TO DO'S
Weekly

MUST DO!

_____

_____

_____

IMPORTANT

- _____
- _____
- _____
- _____
- _____
- _____
- _____
- _____
- _____
- _____

LESS IMPORTANT

- _____
- _____
- _____
- _____
- _____
- _____
- _____
- _____
- _____
- _____

NOTES

_____   _____

_____   _____

_____   _____

_____   _____

> In the power of fixing the attention lies the
> most precious of the intellectual habits.
> — ROBERT HALL

HABIT TRACKER
Weekly

HÁBITS	MON	TUES	WED	THU	FRI	SAT	SUN
	○	○	○	○	○	○	○
	○	○	○	○	○	○	○
	○	○	○	○	○	○	○
	○	○	○	○	○	○	○
	○	○	○	○	○	○	○
	○	○	○	○	○	○	○
	○	○	○	○	○	○	○
	○	○	○	○	○	○	○
	○	○	○	○	○	○	○
	○	○	○	○	○	○	○
	○	○	○	○	○	○	○
	○	○	○	○	○	○	○
	○	○	○	○	○	○	○
	○	○	○	○	○	○	○

HOW DID I DO?

"I have more thoughts before breakfast
than most people have all day."
— UNKNOWN

BRAIN DUMP

Though Organizer

MUST DO	SHOULD DO

COULD START	MUST DO

DAILY PLANNER

TODAY'S GOALS

MOOD:

WATER INTAKE:

PRIORITIES WITH CONSEQUENCES

A⁺

A⁺

THINGS TO GET DONE TODAY:

TODAY'S APPOINTMENT:

A⁺

TIME: EVENT:

FOR TOMORROW:

		1	2	3	4	5	6	7	8	9	10
IMPULSIVITY	Easily Frustrated	1	2	3	4	5	6	7	8	9	10
	Acting Without Thikining	1	2	3	4	5	6	7	8	9	10
	Interrupting Others	1	2	3	4	5	6	7	8	9	10
	Emotional Outbursts	1	2	3	4	5	6	7	8	9	10
HYPERACTIVITY	Difficulty Sleeping	1	2	3	4	5	6	7	8	9	10
	Constantly Moving	1	2	3	4	5	6	7	8	9	10
	Unable to Sit Still / Fidgeting	1	2	3	4	5	6	7	8	9	10
	Excessive Talking	1	2	3	4	5	6	7	8	9	10
INATTENTION	Easily Distracted	1	2	3	4	5	6	7	8	9	10
	Careless Mistakes	1	2	3	4	5	6	7	8	9	10
	Short Attention	1	2	3	4	5	6	7	8	9	10
	Forgetfulness	1	2	3	4	5	6	7	8	9	10

Date _____

DAILY PLANNER

TODAY'S GOALS

MOOD:

😊 🙂 😐 🙁 😢

WATER INTAKE:

💧 💧 💧 💧 💧 💧 💧 💧

PRIORITIES WITH CONSEQUENCES

A⁺

A⁺

A⁺

THINGS TO GET DONE TODAY:

_____
_____
_____
_____
_____
_____
_____
_____

TODAY'S APPOINTMENT:

TIME:	EVENT:

FOR TOMORROW:

_____
_____
_____
_____

		1	2	3	4	5	6	7	8	9	10
IMPULSIVITY	Easily Frustrated	1	2	3	4	5	6	7	8	9	10
	Acting Without Thikining	1	2	3	4	5	6	7	8	9	10
	Interrupting Others	1	2	3	4	5	6	7	8	9	10
	Emotional Outbursts	1	2	3	4	5	6	7	8	9	10
HYPERACTIVITY	Difficulty Sleeping	1	2	3	4	5	6	7	8	9	10
	Constantly Moving	1	2	3	4	5	6	7	8	9	10
	Unable to Sit Still / Fidgeting	1	2	3	4	5	6	7	8	9	10
	Excessive Talking	1	2	3	4	5	6	7	8	9	10
INATTENTION	Easily Distracted	1	2	3	4	5	6	7	8	9	10
	Careless Mistakes	1	2	3	4	5	6	7	8	9	10
	Short Attention	1	2	3	4	5	6	7	8	9	10
	Forgetfulness	1	2	3	4	5	6	7	8	9	10

Date _____

DAILY PLANNER

🎯 TODAY'S GOALS

MOOD:

😊 🙂 😐 🙁 😢

WATER INTAKE:

💧💧💧💧💧💧💧💧

PRIORITIES WITH CONSEQUENCES

A⁺

A⁺

THINGS TO GET DONE TODAY:

_____
_____
_____
_____
_____
_____
_____
_____

TODAY'S APPOINTMENT:

TIME:	EVENT:

A⁺

FOR TOMORROW:

_____
_____
_____
_____

		1	2	3	4	5	6	7	8	9	10
IMPULSIVITY	Easily Frustrated	1	2	3	4	5	6	7	8	9	10
	Acting Without Thikining	1	2	3	4	5	6	7	8	9	10
	Interrupting Others	1	2	3	4	5	6	7	8	9	10
	Emotional Outbursts	1	2	3	4	5	6	7	8	9	10
HYPERACTIVITY	Difficulty Sleeping	1	2	3	4	5	6	7	8	9	10
	Constantly Moving	1	2	3	4	5	6	7	8	9	10
	Unable to Sit Still / Fidgeting	1	2	3	4	5	6	7	8	9	10
	Excessive Talking	1	2	3	4	5	6	7	8	9	10
INATTENTION	Easily Distracted	1	2	3	4	5	6	7	8	9	10
	Careless Mistakes	1	2	3	4	5	6	7	8	9	10
	Short Attention	1	2	3	4	5	6	7	8	9	10
	Forgetfulness	1	2	3	4	5	6	7	8	9	10

Date _____

DAILY PLANNER

Today's goals

Mood:

☺ ☺ ☹ ☹ ☹

Water Intake:

◇◇◇◇◇◇◇◇

Priorities with Consequences

A⁺

A⁺

A⁺

Things to get done today:

_____
_____
_____
_____
_____
_____
_____
_____

Today's appointment:

TIME:	EVENT:

For tomorrow:

_____
_____
_____
_____
_____

		1	2	3	4	5	6	7	8	9	10
IMPULSIVITY	Easily Frustrated	1	2	3	4	5	6	7	8	9	10
	Acting Without Thikining	1	2	3	4	5	6	7	8	9	10
	Interrupting Others	1	2	3	4	5	6	7	8	9	10
	Emotional Outbursts	1	2	3	4	5	6	7	8	9	10
HYPERACTIVITY	Difficulty Sleeping	1	2	3	4	5	6	7	8	9	10
	Constantly Moving	1	2	3	4	5	6	7	8	9	10
	Unable to Sit Still / Fidgeting	1	2	3	4	5	6	7	8	9	10
	Excessive Talking	1	2	3	4	5	6	7	8	9	10
INATTENTION	Easily Distracted	1	2	3	4	5	6	7	8	9	10
	Careless Mistakes	1	2	3	4	5	6	7	8	9	10
	Short Attention	1	2	3	4	5	6	7	8	9	10
	Forgetfulness	1	2	3	4	5	6	7	8	9	10

Date _____

DAILY PLANNER

Today's goals

Mood:

Priorities with Consequences

Water Intake:

| A⁺ |

| A⁺ |

Things to get done today:

_____
_____
_____
_____
_____
_____
_____
_____
_____

Today's appointment:

TIME:	EVENT:

| A⁺ |

For tomorrow:

_____
_____
_____
_____
_____
_____

		1	2	3	4	5	6	7	8	9	10
IMPULSIVITY	Easily Frustrated	1	2	3	4	5	6	7	8	9	10
	Acting Without Thikining	1	2	3	4	5	6	7	8	9	10
	Interrupting Others	1	2	3	4	5	6	7	8	9	10
	Emotional Outbursts	1	2	3	4	5	6	7	8	9	10
HYPERACTIVITY	Difficulty Sleeping	1	2	3	4	5	6	7	8	9	10
	Constantly Moving	1	2	3	4	5	6	7	8	9	10
	Unable to Sit Still / Fidgeting	1	2	3	4	5	6	7	8	9	10
	Excessive Talking	1	2	3	4	5	6	7	8	9	10
INATTENTION	Easily Distracted	1	2	3	4	5	6	7	8	9	10
	Careless Mistakes	1	2	3	4	5	6	7	8	9	10
	Short Attention	1	2	3	4	5	6	7	8	9	10
	Forgetfulness	1	2	3	4	5	6	7	8	9	10

Date _____

DAILY PLANNER

TODAY'S GOALS

MOOD:

WATER INTAKE:

PRIORITIES WITH CONSEQUENCES

A⁺

A⁺

A⁺

THINGS TO GET DONE TODAY:

_____
_____
_____
_____
_____
_____
_____
_____

TODAY'S APPOINTMENT:

TIME: EVENT:

FOR TOMORROW:

_____
_____
_____
_____
_____

		1	2	3	4	5	6	7	8	9	10
IMPULSIVITY	Easily Frustrated	1	2	3	4	5	6	7	8	9	10
	Acting Without Thikining	1	2	3	4	5	6	7	8	9	10
	Interrupting Others	1	2	3	4	5	6	7	8	9	10
	Emotional Outbursts	1	2	3	4	5	6	7	8	9	10
HYPERACTIVITY	Difficulty Sleeping	1	2	3	4	5	6	7	8	9	10
	Constantly Moving	1	2	3	4	5	6	7	8	9	10
	Unable to Sit Still / Fidgeting	1	2	3	4	5	6	7	8	9	10
	Excessive Talking	1	2	3	4	5	6	7	8	9	10
INATTENTION	Easily Distracted	1	2	3	4	5	6	7	8	9	10
	Careless Mistakes	1	2	3	4	5	6	7	8	9	10
	Short Attention	1	2	3	4	5	6	7	8	9	10
	Forgetfulness	1	2	3	4	5	6	7	8	9	10

Date _____

DAILY PLANNER

Today's goals

Mood:

Water Intake:

Priorities with Consequences

A⁺

A⁺

Things to get done today:

_____
_____
_____
_____
_____
_____
_____
_____
_____

Today's appointment:

TIME:	EVENT:

A⁺

For tomorrow:

_____
_____
_____
_____
_____
_____

		1	2	3	4	5	6	7	8	9	10
IMPULSIVITY	Easily Frustrated	1	2	3	4	5	6	7	8	9	10
	Acting Without Thikinig	1	2	3	4	5	6	7	8	9	10
	Interrupting Others	1	2	3	4	5	6	7	8	9	10
	Emotional Outbursts	1	2	3	4	5	6	7	8	9	10
HYPERACTIVITY	Difficulty Sleeping	1	2	3	4	5	6	7	8	9	10
	Constantly Moving	1	2	3	4	5	6	7	8	9	10
	Unable to Sit Still / Fidgeting	1	2	3	4	5	6	7	8	9	10
	Excessive Talking	1	2	3	4	5	6	7	8	9	10
INATTENTION	Easily Distracted	1	2	3	4	5	6	7	8	9	10
	Careless Mistakes	1	2	3	4	5	6	7	8	9	10
	Short Attention	1	2	3	4	5	6	7	8	9	10
	Forgetfulness	1	2	3	4	5	6	7	8	9	10

MEDICATION
Tracker

	MEDICATION	DOSAGE	FREQUENCY	TAKEN
MONDAY				
TUESDAY				
WEDNESDAY				
THURSDAY				
FRIDAY				
SATURDAY				
SUNDAY				

NOTES

TO DO'S
Weekly

MUST DO!

_____
_____
_____

IMPORTANT

- _____
- _____
- _____
- _____
- _____
- _____
- _____
- _____
- _____
- _____

LESS IMPORTANT

- _____
- _____
- _____
- _____
- _____
- _____
- _____
- _____
- _____
- _____

NOTES

_____   _____
_____   _____
_____   _____
_____   _____

In the power of fixing the attention lies the
most precious of the intellectual habits.
— Robert Hall

HABIT TRACKER
Weekly

HÁBITS	MON	TUES	WED	THU	FRI	SAT	SUN
_____	◯	◯	◯	◯	◯	◯	◯
_____	◯	◯	◯	◯	◯	◯	◯
_____	◯	◯	◯	◯	◯	◯	◯
_____	◯	◯	◯	◯	◯	◯	◯
_____	◯	◯	◯	◯	◯	◯	◯
_____	◯	◯	◯	◯	◯	◯	◯
_____	◯	◯	◯	◯	◯	◯	◯
_____	◯	◯	◯	◯	◯	◯	◯
_____	◯	◯	◯	◯	◯	◯	◯
_____	◯	◯	◯	◯	◯	◯	◯
_____	◯	◯	◯	◯	◯	◯	◯
_____	◯	◯	◯	◯	◯	◯	◯
_____	◯	◯	◯	◯	◯	◯	◯
_____	◯	◯	◯	◯	◯	◯	◯

HOW DID I DO?

"I have more thoughts before breakfast
than most people have all day."
— UNKNOWN

BRAIN DUMP

Though Organizer

MUST DO	SHOULD DO

COULD START	MUST DO

DAILY PLANNER

Today's Goals

Mood:

Water Intake:

Priorities with Consequences

A⁺

A⁺

A⁺

Things to get done today:

_____
_____
_____
_____
_____
_____
_____

Today's Appointment:

TIME:	EVENT:

For Tomorrow:

_____
_____
_____
_____
_____

		1	2	3	4	5	6	7	8	9	10
IMPULSIVITY	Easily Frustrated	1	2	3	4	5	6	7	8	9	10
	Acting Without Thikining	1	2	3	4	5	6	7	8	9	10
	Interrupting Others	1	2	3	4	5	6	7	8	9	10
	Emotional Outbursts	1	2	3	4	5	6	7	8	9	10
HYPERACTIVITY	Difficulty Sleeping	1	2	3	4	5	6	7	8	9	10
	Constantly Moving	1	2	3	4	5	6	7	8	9	10
	Unable to Sit Still / Fidgeting	1	2	3	4	5	6	7	8	9	10
	Excessive Talking	1	2	3	4	5	6	7	8	9	10
INATTENTION	Easily Distracted	1	2	3	4	5	6	7	8	9	10
	Careless Mistakes	1	2	3	4	5	6	7	8	9	10
	Short Attention	1	2	3	4	5	6	7	8	9	10
	Forgetfulness	1	2	3	4	5	6	7	8	9	10

DAILY PLANNER

Today's Goals

Mood:

😄 🙂 😐 🙁 😣

Water Intake:

💧💧💧💧💧💧💧💧

Priorities with Consequences

A⁺

A⁺

A⁺

Things to get done today:

_____
_____
_____
_____
_____
_____
_____
_____

Today's appointment:

Time:	Event:

For tomorrow:

_____
_____
_____
_____
_____

		1	2	3	4	5	6	7	8	9	10
IMPULSIVITY	Easily Frustrated	1	2	3	4	5	6	7	8	9	10
	Acting Without Thikining	1	2	3	4	5	6	7	8	9	10
	Interrupting Others	1	2	3	4	5	6	7	8	9	10
	Emotional Outbursts	1	2	3	4	5	6	7	8	9	10
HYPERACTIVITY	Difficulty Sleeping	1	2	3	4	5	6	7	8	9	10
	Constantly Moving	1	2	3	4	5	6	7	8	9	10
	Unable to Sit Still / Fidgeting	1	2	3	4	5	6	7	8	9	10
	Excessive Talking	1	2	3	4	5	6	7	8	9	10
INATTENTION	Easily Distracted	1	2	3	4	5	6	7	8	9	10
	Careless Mistakes	1	2	3	4	5	6	7	8	9	10
	Short Attention	1	2	3	4	5	6	7	8	9	10
	Forgetfulness	1	2	3	4	5	6	7	8	9	10

DAILY PLANNER

🎯 TODAY'S GOALS

MOOD:

😊 🙂 😐 🙁 😢

WATER INTAKE:

💧 💧 💧 💧 💧 💧 💧

PRIORITIES WITH CONSEQUENCES

A⁺

A⁺

THINGS TO GET DONE TODAY:

_____
_____
_____
_____
_____
_____
_____
_____

TODAY'S APPOINTMENT:

TIME:	EVENT:

A⁺

FOR TOMORROW:

_____
_____
_____
_____
_____

		1	2	3	4	5	6	7	8	9	10
IMPULSIVITY	Easily Frustrated	1	2	3	4	5	6	7	8	9	10
	Acting Without Thikining	1	2	3	4	5	6	7	8	9	10
	Interrupting Others	1	2	3	4	5	6	7	8	9	10
	Emotional Outbursts	1	2	3	4	5	6	7	8	9	10
HYPERACTIVITY	Difficulty Sleeping	1	2	3	4	5	6	7	8	9	10
	Constantly Moving	1	2	3	4	5	6	7	8	9	10
	Unable to Sit Still / Fidgeting	1	2	3	4	5	6	7	8	9	10
	Excessive Talking	1	2	3	4	5	6	7	8	9	10
INATTENTION	Easily Distracted	1	2	3	4	5	6	7	8	9	10
	Careless Mistakes	1	2	3	4	5	6	7	8	9	10
	Short Attention	1	2	3	4	5	6	7	8	9	10
	Forgetfulness	1	2	3	4	5	6	7	8	9	10

Date  _____

DAILY PLANNER

Today's goals

Mood:

😄 🙂 😐 🙁 😢

Water Intake:

💧💧💧💧💧💧💧💧

Priorities with Consequences

A⁺

A⁺

A⁺

Things to get done today:

_____
_____
_____
_____
_____
_____
_____

Today's appointment:

TIME:	EVENT:

For tomorrow:

_____
_____
_____
_____
_____

		1	2	3	4	5	6	7	8	9	10
IMPULSIVITY	Easily Frustrated	1	2	3	4	5	6	7	8	9	10
	Acting Without Thikining	1	2	3	4	5	6	7	8	9	10
	Interrupting Others	1	2	3	4	5	6	7	8	9	10
	Emotional Outbursts	1	2	3	4	5	6	7	8	9	10
HYPERACTIVITY	Difficulty Sleeping	1	2	3	4	5	6	7	8	9	10
	Constantly Moving	1	2	3	4	5	6	7	8	9	10
	Unable to Sit Still / Fidgeting	1	2	3	4	5	6	7	8	9	10
	Excessive Talking	1	2	3	4	5	6	7	8	9	10
INATTENTION	Easily Distracted	1	2	3	4	5	6	7	8	9	10
	Careless Mistakes	1	2	3	4	5	6	7	8	9	10
	Short Attention	1	2	3	4	5	6	7	8	9	10
	Forgetfulness	1	2	3	4	5	6	7	8	9	10

Date _____

DAILY PLANNER

Today's goals

Mood:

😄 🙂 😐 🙁 😞

Water Intake:

⬭⬭⬭⬭⬭⬭⬭⬭

Priorities with Consequences

A⁺

A⁺

A⁺

Things to get done today:

_____
_____
_____
_____
_____
_____
_____
_____

Today's appointment:

TIME:	EVENT:

For tomorrow:

_____
_____
_____
_____
_____

		1	2	3	4	5	6	7	8	9	10
IMPULSIVITY	Easily Frustrated	1	2	3	4	5	6	7	8	9	10
	Acting Without Thikining	1	2	3	4	5	6	7	8	9	10
	Interrupting Others	1	2	3	4	5	6	7	8	9	10
	Emotional Outbursts	1	2	3	4	5	6	7	8	9	10
HYPERACTIVITY	Difficulty Sleeping	1	2	3	4	5	6	7	8	9	10
	Constantly Moving	1	2	3	4	5	6	7	8	9	10
	Unable to Sit Still / Fidgeting	1	2	3	4	5	6	7	8	9	10
	Excessive Talking	1	2	3	4	5	6	7	8	9	10
INATTENTION	Easily Distracted	1	2	3	4	5	6	7	8	9	10
	Careless Mistakes	1	2	3	4	5	6	7	8	9	10
	Short Attention	1	2	3	4	5	6	7	8	9	10
	Forgetfulness	1	2	3	4	5	6	7	8	9	10

Date _____

DAILY PLANNER

Today's goals

Mood:

😊 🙂 😐 🙁 😰

Water Intake:

💧💧💧💧💧💧💧💧

Priorities with Consequences

A⁺

A⁺

Things to get done today:

_____
_____
_____
_____
_____
_____
_____

Today's appointment:

TIME:	EVENT:

A⁺

For tomorrow:

_____
_____
_____
_____

		1	2	3	4	5	6	7	8	9	10
IMPULSIVITY	Easily Frustrated	1	2	3	4	5	6	7	8	9	10
	Acting Without Thikining	1	2	3	4	5	6	7	8	9	10
	Interrupting Others	1	2	3	4	5	6	7	8	9	10
	Emotional Outbursts	1	2	3	4	5	6	7	8	9	10
HYPERACTIVITY	Difficulty Sleeping	1	2	3	4	5	6	7	8	9	10
	Constantly Moving	1	2	3	4	5	6	7	8	9	10
	Unable to Sit Still / Fidgeting	1	2	3	4	5	6	7	8	9	10
	Excessive Talking	1	2	3	4	5	6	7	8	9	10
INATTENTION	Easily Distracted	1	2	3	4	5	6	7	8	9	10
	Careless Mistakes	1	2	3	4	5	6	7	8	9	10
	Short Attention	1	2	3	4	5	6	7	8	9	10
	Forgetfulness	1	2	3	4	5	6	7	8	9	10

 Date _____

DAILY PLANNER

Today's goals

Mood:

Priorities with Consequences

A⁺

Water Intake:

A⁺

Things to get done today:

Today's appointment:

A⁺

TIME:	EVENT:

For tomorrow:

		1	2	3	4	5	6	7	8	9	10
IMPULSIVITY	Easily Frustrated	1	2	3	4	5	6	7	8	9	10
	Acting Without Thikining	1	2	3	4	5	6	7	8	9	10
	Interrupting Others	1	2	3	4	5	6	7	8	9	10
	Emotional Outbursts	1	2	3	4	5	6	7	8	9	10
HYPERACTIVITY	Difficulty Sleeping	1	2	3	4	5	6	7	8	9	10
	Constantly Moving	1	2	3	4	5	6	7	8	9	10
	Unable to Sit Still / Fidgeting	1	2	3	4	5	6	7	8	9	10
	Excessive Talking	1	2	3	4	5	6	7	8	9	10
INATTENTION	Easily Distracted	1	2	3	4	5	6	7	8	9	10
	Careless Mistakes	1	2	3	4	5	6	7	8	9	10
	Short Attention	1	2	3	4	5	6	7	8	9	10
	Forgetfulness	1	2	3	4	5	6	7	8	9	10

MEDICATION
Tracker

	MEDICATION	DOSAGE	FREQUENCY	TAKEN
MONDAY				
TUESDAY				
WEDNESDAY				
THURSDAY				
FRIDAY				
SATURDAY				
SUNDAY				

NOTES

Nothing like ADHD and a good
fight to the death to make time fly.

—RICK RIORDAN

TO DO'S
Weekly

MUST DO!

_____
_____
_____
_____

IMPORTANT

- _____
- _____
- _____
- _____
- _____
- _____
- _____
- _____
- _____
- _____

LESS IMPORTANT

- _____
- _____
- _____
- _____
- _____
- _____
- _____
- _____
- _____
- _____

NOTES

_____ _____
_____ _____
_____ _____
_____ _____

In the power of fixing the attention lies the
most precious of the intellectual habits.
– ROBERT HALL

HABIT TRACKER
Weekly

HÁBITS	MON	TUES	WED	THU	FRI	SAT	SUN
	○	○	○	○	○	○	○
	○	○	○	○	○	○	○
	○	○	○	○	○	○	○
	○	○	○	○	○	○	○
	○	○	○	○	○	○	○
	○	○	○	○	○	○	○
	○	○	○	○	○	○	○
	○	○	○	○	○	○	○
	○	○	○	○	○	○	○
	○	○	○	○	○	○	○
	○	○	○	○	○	○	○
	○	○	○	○	○	○	○
	○	○	○	○	○	○	○
	○	○	○	○	○	○	○

HOW DID I DO?

"I have more thoughts before breakfast
than most people have all day."
— UNKNOWN

BRAIN DUMP

Though Organizer

MUST DO	SHOULD DO
COULD START	MUST DO

DAILY PLANNER

TODAY'S GOALS

MOOD:

PRIORITIES WITH CONSEQUENCES

WATER INTAKE:

THINGS TO GET DONE TODAY:

_____
_____
_____
_____
_____
_____
_____
_____
_____
_____
_____

TODAY'S APPOINTMENT:

TIME:	EVENT:

FOR TOMORROW:

_____
_____
_____
_____
_____

		1	2	3	4	5	6	7	8	9	10
IMPULSIVITY	Easily Frustrated	1	2	3	4	5	6	7	8	9	10
	Acting Without Thikining	1	2	3	4	5	6	7	8	9	10
	Interrupting Others	1	2	3	4	5	6	7	8	9	10
	Emotional Outbursts	1	2	3	4	5	6	7	8	9	10
HYPERACTIVITY	Difficulty Sleeping	1	2	3	4	5	6	7	8	9	10
	Constantly Moving	1	2	3	4	5	6	7	8	9	10
	Unable to Sit Still / Fidgeting	1	2	3	4	5	6	7	8	9	10
	Excessive Talking	1	2	3	4	5	6	7	8	9	10
INATTENTION	Easily Distracted	1	2	3	4	5	6	7	8	9	10
	Careless Mistakes	1	2	3	4	5	6	7	8	9	10
	Short Attention	1	2	3	4	5	6	7	8	9	10
	Forgetfulness	1	2	3	4	5	6	7	8	9	10

Date _____

DAILY PLANNER

Today's goals

Mood:

Water Intake:

Priorities with Consequences

A^+

A^+

A^+

Things to get done today:

_____
_____
_____
_____
_____
_____
_____
_____
_____

Today's appointment:

TIME:	EVENT:

For tomorrow:

_____
_____
_____
_____
_____

		1	2	3	4	5	6	7	8	9	10
IMPULSIVITY	Easily Frustrated	1	2	3	4	5	6	7	8	9	10
	Acting Without Thikining	1	2	3	4	5	6	7	8	9	10
	Interrupting Others	1	2	3	4	5	6	7	8	9	10
	Emotional Outbursts	1	2	3	4	5	6	7	8	9	10
HYPERACTIVITY	Difficulty Sleeping	1	2	3	4	5	6	7	8	9	10
	Constantly Moving	1	2	3	4	5	6	7	8	9	10
	Unable to Sit Still / Fidgeting	1	2	3	4	5	6	7	8	9	10
	Excessive Talking	1	2	3	4	5	6	7	8	9	10
INATTENTION	Easily Distracted	1	2	3	4	5	6	7	8	9	10
	Careless Mistakes	1	2	3	4	5	6	7	8	9	10
	Short Attention	1	2	3	4	5	6	7	8	9	10
	Forgetfulness	1	2	3	4	5	6	7	8	9	10

 *Date* _____

DAILY PLANNER

Today's goals

Mood:

🙂 🙂 😐 🙁 ☹️

Water Intake:

💧 💧 💧 💧 💧 💧 💧

Priorities with Consequences

A⁺

A⁺

A⁺

Things to get done today:

_____
_____
_____
_____
_____
_____
_____

Today's appointment:

TIME:	EVENT:

For tomorrow:

_____
_____
_____
_____
_____

		1	2	3	4	5	6	7	8	9	10
IMPULSIVITY	Easily Frustrated	1	2	3	4	5	6	7	8	9	10
	Acting Without Thikining	1	2	3	4	5	6	7	8	9	10
	Interrupting Others	1	2	3	4	5	6	7	8	9	10
	Emotional Outbursts	1	2	3	4	5	6	7	8	9	10
HYPERACTIVITY	Difficulty Sleeping	1	2	3	4	5	6	7	8	9	10
	Constantly Moving	1	2	3	4	5	6	7	8	9	10
	Unable to Sit Still / Fidgeting	1	2	3	4	5	6	7	8	9	10
	Excessive Talking	1	2	3	4	5	6	7	8	9	10
INATTENTION	Easily Distracted	1	2	3	4	5	6	7	8	9	10
	Careless Mistakes	1	2	3	4	5	6	7	8	9	10
	Short Attention	1	2	3	4	5	6	7	8	9	10
	Forgetfulness	1	2	3	4	5	6	7	8	9	10

DAILY PLANNER

TODAY'S GOALS

MOOD:

😊 🙂 😐 🙁 😢

WATER INTAKE:

💧💧💧💧💧💧💧💧💧

PRIORITIES WITH CONSEQUENCES

A⁺

A⁺

A⁺

THINGS TO GET DONE TODAY:

_____
_____
_____
_____
_____
_____
_____
_____

TODAY'S APPOINTMENT:

TIME:	EVENT:

FOR TOMORROW:

_____
_____
_____
_____
_____

		1	2	3	4	5	6	7	8	9	10
IMPULSIVITY	Easily Frustrated	1	2	3	4	5	6	7	8	9	10
	Acting Without Thikining	1	2	3	4	5	6	7	8	9	10
	Interrupting Others	1	2	3	4	5	6	7	8	9	10
	Emotional Outbursts	1	2	3	4	5	6	7	8	9	10
HYPERACTIVITY	Difficulty Sleeping	1	2	3	4	5	6	7	8	9	10
	Constantly Moving	1	2	3	4	5	6	7	8	9	10
	Unable to Sit Still / Fidgeting	1	2	3	4	5	6	7	8	9	10
	Excessive Talking	1	2	3	4	5	6	7	8	9	10
INATTENTION	Easily Distracted	1	2	3	4	5	6	7	8	9	10
	Careless Mistakes	1	2	3	4	5	6	7	8	9	10
	Short Attention	1	2	3	4	5	6	7	8	9	10
	Forgetfulness	1	2	3	4	5	6	7	8	9	10

DAILY PLANNER

TODAY'S GOALS

MOOD:

WATER INTAKE:

PRIORITIES WITH CONSEQUENCES

A⁺

A⁺

THINGS TO GET DONE TODAY:

TODAY'S APPOINTMENT:

A⁺

TIME: EVENT:

FOR TOMORROW:

		1	2	3	4	5	6	7	8	9	10
IMPULSIVITY	Easily Frustrated	1	2	3	4	5	6	7	8	9	10
	Acting Without Thikining	1	2	3	4	5	6	7	8	9	10
	Interrupting Others	1	2	3	4	5	6	7	8	9	10
	Emotional Outbursts	1	2	3	4	5	6	7	8	9	10
HYPERACTIVITY	Difficulty Sleeping	1	2	3	4	5	6	7	8	9	10
	Constantly Moving	1	2	3	4	5	6	7	8	9	10
	Unable to Sit Still / Fidgeting	1	2	3	4	5	6	7	8	9	10
	Excessive Talking	1	2	3	4	5	6	7	8	9	10
INATTENTION	Easily Distracted	1	2	3	4	5	6	7	8	9	10
	Careless Mistakes	1	2	3	4	5	6	7	8	9	10
	Short Attention	1	2	3	4	5	6	7	8	9	10
	Forgetfulness	1	2	3	4	5	6	7	8	9	10

DAILY PLANNER

TODAY'S GOALS

MOOD:

😊 🙂 😐 🙁 😢

WATER INTAKE:

◇ ◇ ◇ ◇ ◇ ◇ ◇ ◇

PRIORITIES WITH CONSEQUENCES

A⁺

A⁺

A⁺

THINGS TO GET DONE TODAY:

_____
_____
_____
_____
_____
_____
_____
_____

TODAY'S APPOINTMENT:

TIME:	EVENT:

FOR TOMORROW:

_____
_____
_____
_____
_____

		1	2	3	4	5	6	7	8	9	10
IMPULSIVITY	Easily Frustrated	1	2	3	4	5	6	7	8	9	10
	Acting Without Thikining	1	2	3	4	5	6	7	8	9	10
	Interrupting Others	1	2	3	4	5	6	7	8	9	10
	Emotional Outbursts	1	2	3	4	5	6	7	8	9	10
HYPERACTIVITY	Difficulty Sleeping	1	2	3	4	5	6	7	8	9	10
	Constantly Moving	1	2	3	4	5	6	7	8	9	10
	Unable to Sit Still / Fidgeting	1	2	3	4	5	6	7	8	9	10
	Excessive Talking	1	2	3	4	5	6	7	8	9	10
INATTENTION	Easily Distracted	1	2	3	4	5	6	7	8	9	10
	Careless Mistakes	1	2	3	4	5	6	7	8	9	10
	Short Attention	1	2	3	4	5	6	7	8	9	10
	Forgetfulness	1	2	3	4	5	6	7	8	9	10

 Date _____

DAILY PLANNER

Today's goals

Mood:

Priorities with Consequences

A⁺

Water Intake:

A⁺

Things to get done today:

_____
_____
_____
_____
_____
_____
_____
_____
_____

Today's appointment:

A⁺

TIME:	EVENT:

For tomorrow:

_____
_____
_____
_____
_____

IMPULSIVITY	Easily Frustrated	1	2	3	4	5	6	7	8	9	10
	Acting Without Thikining	1	2	3	4	5	6	7	8	9	10
	Interrupting Others	1	2	3	4	5	6	7	8	9	10
	Emotional Outbursts	1	2	3	4	5	6	7	8	9	10
HYPERACTIVITY	Difficulty Sleeping	1	2	3	4	5	6	7	8	9	10
	Constantly Moving	1	2	3	4	5	6	7	8	9	10
	Unable to Sit Still / Fidgeting	1	2	3	4	5	6	7	8	9	10
	Excessive Talking	1	2	3	4	5	6	7	8	9	10
INATTENTION	Easily Distracted	1	2	3	4	5	6	7	8	9	10
	Careless Mistakes	1	2	3	4	5	6	7	8	9	10
	Short Attention	1	2	3	4	5	6	7	8	9	10
	Forgetfulness	1	2	3	4	5	6	7	8	9	10

MEDICATION
Tracker

	MEDICATION	DOSAGE	FREQUENCY	TAKEN
MONDAY				
TUESDAY				
WEDNESDAY				
THURSDAY				
FRIDAY				
SATURDAY				
SUNDAY				

NOTES

Nothing like ADHD and a good
fight to the death to make time fly.

—RICK RIORDAN

TO DO'S
Weekly

MUST DO!

_____

_____

_____

IMPORTANT

- _____
- _____
- _____
- _____
- _____
- _____
- _____
- _____
- _____
- _____

LESS IMPORTANT

- _____
- _____
- _____
- _____
- _____
- _____
- _____
- _____
- _____
- _____

NOTES

_____   _____

_____   _____

_____   _____

In the power of fixing the attention lies the
most precious of the intellectual habits.
— ROBERT HALL

HABIT TRACKER
Weekly

HÁBITS	MON	TUES	WED	THU	FRI	SAT	SUN
_____	○	○	○	○	○	○	○
_____	○	○	○	○	○	○	○
_____	○	○	○	○	○	○	○
_____	○	○	○	○	○	○	○
_____	○	○	○	○	○	○	○
_____	○	○	○	○	○	○	○
_____	○	○	○	○	○	○	○
_____	○	○	○	○	○	○	○
_____	○	○	○	○	○	○	○
_____	○	○	○	○	○	○	○
_____	○	○	○	○	○	○	○
_____	○	○	○	○	○	○	○
_____	○	○	○	○	○	○	○
_____	○	○	○	○	○	○	○

HOW DID I DO?

*"I have more thoughts before breakfast
than most people have all day."*
— UNKNOWN

BRAIN DUMP
Though Organizer

MUST DO	SHOULD DO

COULD START	MUST DO

Date _____

DAILY PLANNER

Today's goals

Mood:
😊 🙂 😐 🙁 ☹️

Water Intake:
💧 💧 💧 💧 💧 💧 💧 💧

Priorities with Consequences

A⁺

A⁺

Things to get done today:
_____
_____
_____
_____
_____
_____
_____
_____
_____

Today's appointment:

TIME:	EVENT:

A⁺

For tomorrow:
_____
_____
_____
_____
_____

		1	2	3	4	5	6	7	8	9	10
IMPULSIVITY	Easily Frustrated	1	2	3	4	5	6	7	8	9	10
	Acting Without Thikining	1	2	3	4	5	6	7	8	9	10
	Interrupting Others	1	2	3	4	5	6	7	8	9	10
	Emotional Outbursts	1	2	3	4	5	6	7	8	9	10
HYPERACTIVITY	Difficulty Sleeping	1	2	3	4	5	6	7	8	9	10
	Constantly Moving	1	2	3	4	5	6	7	8	9	10
	Unable to Sit Still / Fidgeting	1	2	3	4	5	6	7	8	9	10
	Excessive Talking	1	2	3	4	5	6	7	8	9	10
INATTENTION	Easily Distracted	1	2	3	4	5	6	7	8	9	10
	Careless Mistakes	1	2	3	4	5	6	7	8	9	10
	Short Attention	1	2	3	4	5	6	7	8	9	10
	Forgetfulness	1	2	3	4	5	6	7	8	9	10

Date _____

DAILY PLANNER

Today's Goals

Mood:

😄 🙂 😐 🙁 😢

Water Intake:

⬥ ⬥ ⬥ ⬥ ⬥ ⬥ ⬥

Priorities with Consequences

A⁺

A⁺

A⁺

Things to get done today:

_____
_____
_____
_____
_____
_____
_____
_____

Today's appointment:

TIME:	EVENT:

For tomorrow:

_____
_____
_____
_____
_____

		1	2	3	4	5	6	7	8	9	10
IMPULSIVITY	Easily Frustrated	1	2	3	4	5	6	7	8	9	10
	Acting Without Thiking	1	2	3	4	5	6	7	8	9	10
	Interrupting Others	1	2	3	4	5	6	7	8	9	10
	Emotional Outbursts	1	2	3	4	5	6	7	8	9	10
HYPERACTIVITY	Difficulty Sleeping	1	2	3	4	5	6	7	8	9	10
	Constantly Moving	1	2	3	4	5	6	7	8	9	10
	Unable to Sit Still / Fidgeting	1	2	3	4	5	6	7	8	9	10
	Excessive Talking	1	2	3	4	5	6	7	8	9	10
INATTENTION	Easily Distracted	1	2	3	4	5	6	7	8	9	10
	Careless Mistakes	1	2	3	4	5	6	7	8	9	10
	Short Attention	1	2	3	4	5	6	7	8	9	10
	Forgetfulness	1	2	3	4	5	6	7	8	9	10

Date _____

DAILY PLANNER

Today's goals

Mood:

🙂 🙂 😐 🙁 😢

Priorities with Consequences

A⁺

Water Intake:

⬦ ⬦ ⬦ ⬦ ⬦ ⬦ ⬦ ⬦

A⁺

Things to get done today:

Today's appointment:

A⁺

TIME:	EVENT:

For tomorrow:

		1	2	3	4	5	6	7	8	9	10
IMPULSIVITY	Easily Frustrated	1	2	3	4	5	6	7	8	9	10
	Acting Without Thikining	1	2	3	4	5	6	7	8	9	10
	Interrupting Others	1	2	3	4	5	6	7	8	9	10
	Emotional Outbursts	1	2	3	4	5	6	7	8	9	10
HYPERACTIVITY	Difficulty Sleeping	1	2	3	4	5	6	7	8	9	10
	Constantly Moving	1	2	3	4	5	6	7	8	9	10
	Unable to Sit Still / Fidgeting	1	2	3	4	5	6	7	8	9	10
	Excessive Talking	1	2	3	4	5	6	7	8	9	10
INATTENTION	Easily Distracted	1	2	3	4	5	6	7	8	9	10
	Careless Mistakes	1	2	3	4	5	6	7	8	9	10
	Short Attention	1	2	3	4	5	6	7	8	9	10
	Forgetfulness	1	2	3	4	5	6	7	8	9	10

Date _____

DAILY PLANNER

Today's goals

Mood:

🙂 🙂 😐 🙁 😞

Water Intake:

💧💧💧💧💧💧💧💧

Priorities with Consequences

A⁺

A⁺

A⁺

Things to get done today:

_____
_____
_____
_____
_____
_____
_____
_____
_____

Today's appointment:

TIME:	EVENT:

For tomorrow:

_____
_____
_____
_____
_____
_____

IMPULSIVITY	Easily Frustrated	1	2	3	4	5	6	7	8	9	10
	Acting Without Thikining	1	2	3	4	5	6	7	8	9	10
	Interrupting Others	1	2	3	4	5	6	7	8	9	10
	Emotional Outbursts	1	2	3	4	5	6	7	8	9	10
HYPERACTIVITY	Difficulty Sleeping	1	2	3	4	5	6	7	8	9	10
	Constantly Moving	1	2	3	4	5	6	7	8	9	10
	Unable to Sit Still / Fidgeting	1	2	3	4	5	6	7	8	9	10
	Excessive Talking	1	2	3	4	5	6	7	8	9	10
INATTENTION	Easily Distracted	1	2	3	4	5	6	7	8	9	10
	Careless Mistakes	1	2	3	4	5	6	7	8	9	10
	Short Attention	1	2	3	4	5	6	7	8	9	10
	Forgetfulness	1	2	3	4	5	6	7	8	9	10

DAILY PLANNER

Today's goals

Mood:

Water Intake:

Priorities with Consequences

A⁺

A⁺

A⁺

Things to get done today:

Today's appointment:

TIME: EVENT:

For tomorrow:

		1	2	3	4	5	6	7	8	9	10
Impulsivity	Easily Frustrated	1	2	3	4	5	6	7	8	9	10
	Acting Without Thikining	1	2	3	4	5	6	7	8	9	10
	Interrupting Others	1	2	3	4	5	6	7	8	9	10
	Emotional Outbursts	1	2	3	4	5	6	7	8	9	10
Hyperactivity	Difficulty Sleeping	1	2	3	4	5	6	7	8	9	10
	Constantly Moving	1	2	3	4	5	6	7	8	9	10
	Unable to Sit Still / Fidgeting	1	2	3	4	5	6	7	8	9	10
	Excessive Talking	1	2	3	4	5	6	7	8	9	10
Inattention	Easily Distracted	1	2	3	4	5	6	7	8	9	10
	Careless Mistakes	1	2	3	4	5	6	7	8	9	10
	Short Attention	1	2	3	4	5	6	7	8	9	10
	Forgetfulness	1	2	3	4	5	6	7	8	9	10

DAILY PLANNER

Today's goals

Mood:

Water Intake:

Priorities with Consequences

A⁺

A⁺

A⁺

Things to get done today:

Today's appointment:

TIME:	EVENT:

For tomorrow:

		Easily Frustrated	1	2	3	4	5	6	7	8	9	10
IMPULSIVITY		Acting Without Thiking	1	2	3	4	5	6	7	8	9	10
		Interrupting Others	1	2	3	4	5	6	7	8	9	10
		Emotional Outbursts	1	2	3	4	5	6	7	8	9	10
HYPERACTIVITY		Difficulty Sleeping	1	2	3	4	5	6	7	8	9	10
		Constantly Moving	1	2	3	4	5	6	7	8	9	10
		Unable to Sit Still / Fidgeting	1	2	3	4	5	6	7	8	9	10
		Excessive Talking	1	2	3	4	5	6	7	8	9	10
INATTENTION		Easily Distracted	1	2	3	4	5	6	7	8	9	10
		Careless Mistakes	1	2	3	4	5	6	7	8	9	10
		Short Attention	1	2	3	4	5	6	7	8	9	10
		Forgetfulness	1	2	3	4	5	6	7	8	9	10

DAILY PLANNER

Today's goals

Mood:

Water Intake:

Priorities with Consequences

A⁺

A⁺

A⁺

Things to get done today:

_____
_____
_____
_____
_____
_____
_____

Today's appointment:

TIME:	EVENT:

For tomorrow:

_____
_____
_____
_____
_____

		1	2	3	4	5	6	7	8	9	10
IMPULSIVITY	Easily Frustrated	1	2	3	4	5	6	7	8	9	10
	Acting Without Thikining	1	2	3	4	5	6	7	8	9	10
	Interrupting Others	1	2	3	4	5	6	7	8	9	10
	Emotional Outbursts	1	2	3	4	5	6	7	8	9	10
HYPERACTIVITY	Difficulty Sleeping	1	2	3	4	5	6	7	8	9	10
	Constantly Moving	1	2	3	4	5	6	7	8	9	10
	Unable to Sit Still / Fidgeting	1	2	3	4	5	6	7	8	9	10
	Excessive Talking	1	2	3	4	5	6	7	8	9	10
INATTENTION	Easily Distracted	1	2	3	4	5	6	7	8	9	10
	Careless Mistakes	1	2	3	4	5	6	7	8	9	10
	Short Attention	1	2	3	4	5	6	7	8	9	10
	Forgetfulness	1	2	3	4	5	6	7	8	9	10

"It's like being a cat with 100 people with
laser pointers."
— JAMIE HYNDS

MEDICATION
Tracker

	MEDICATION	DOSAGE	FREQUENCY	TAKEN
MONDAY				
TUESDAY				
WEDNESDAY				
THURSDAY				
FRIDAY				
SATURDAY				
SUNDAY				

NOTES

Nothing like ADHD and a good
fight to the death to make time fly.
—RICK RIORDAN

TO DO'S
Weekly

MUST DO!

_____
_____
_____

IMPORTANT

LESS IMPORTANT

NOTES

_____ _____
_____ _____
_____ _____
_____ _____

In the power of fixing the attention lies the
most precious of the intellectual habits.
– ROBERT HALL

HABIT TRACKER
Weekly

HÁBITS	MON	TUES	WED	THU	FRI	SAT	SUN
	○	○	○	○	○	○	○
	○	○	○	○	○	○	○
	○	○	○	○	○	○	○
	○	○	○	○	○	○	○
	○	○	○	○	○	○	○
	○	○	○	○	○	○	○
	○	○	○	○	○	○	○
	○	○	○	○	○	○	○
	○	○	○	○	○	○	○
	○	○	○	○	○	○	○
	○	○	○	○	○	○	○
	○	○	○	○	○	○	○
	○	○	○	○	○	○	○
	○	○	○	○	○	○	○

HOW DID I DO?

"I have more thoughts before breakfast
than most people have all day."
— UNKNOWN

BRAIN DUMP

Though Organizer

MUST DO	SHOULD DO

COULD START	MUST DO

DAILY PLANNER

Today's goals

Mood:

Water Intake:

Priorities with Consequences

A⁺

A⁺

A⁺

Things to get done today:

_____
_____
_____
_____
_____
_____
_____
_____
_____

Today's appointment:

TIME:	EVENT:

For tomorrow:

_____
_____
_____
_____
_____
_____

		1	2	3	4	5	6	7	8	9	10
IMPULSIVITY	Easily Frustrated	1	2	3	4	5	6	7	8	9	10
	Acting Without Thikining	1	2	3	4	5	6	7	8	9	10
	Interrupting Others	1	2	3	4	5	6	7	8	9	10
	Emotional Outbursts	1	2	3	4	5	6	7	8	9	10
HYPERACTIVITY	Difficulty Sleeping	1	2	3	4	5	6	7	8	9	10
	Constantly Moving	1	2	3	4	5	6	7	8	9	10
	Unable to Sit Still / Fidgeting	1	2	3	4	5	6	7	8	9	10
	Excessive Talking	1	2	3	4	5	6	7	8	9	10
INATTENTION	Easily Distracted	1	2	3	4	5	6	7	8	9	10
	Careless Mistakes	1	2	3	4	5	6	7	8	9	10
	Short Attention	1	2	3	4	5	6	7	8	9	10
	Forgetfulness	1	2	3	4	5	6	7	8	9	10

DAILY PLANNER

Today's goals

Mood:

Water Intake:

Priorities with Consequences

A⁺

A⁺

A⁺

Things to get done today:

_____
_____
_____
_____
_____
_____
_____
_____

Today's appointment:

TIME:	EVENT:

For tomorrow:

_____
_____
_____
_____
_____

		1	2	3	4	5	6	7	8	9	10
IMPULSIVITY	Easily Frustrated	1	2	3	4	5	6	7	8	9	10
	Acting Without Thikining	1	2	3	4	5	6	7	8	9	10
	Interrupting Others	1	2	3	4	5	6	7	8	9	10
	Emotional Outbursts	1	2	3	4	5	6	7	8	9	10
HYPERACTIVITY	Difficulty Sleeping	1	2	3	4	5	6	7	8	9	10
	Constantly Moving	1	2	3	4	5	6	7	8	9	10
	Unable to Sit Still / Fidgeting	1	2	3	4	5	6	7	8	9	10
	Excessive Talking	1	2	3	4	5	6	7	8	9	10
INATTENTION	Easily Distracted	1	2	3	4	5	6	7	8	9	10
	Careless Mistakes	1	2	3	4	5	6	7	8	9	10
	Short Attention	1	2	3	4	5	6	7	8	9	10
	Forgetfulness	1	2	3	4	5	6	7	8	9	10

DAILY PLANNER

🎯 TODAY'S GOALS

MOOD:

😊 🙂 😐 🙁 😞

WATER INTAKE:

💧💧💧💧💧💧💧💧

PRIORITIES WITH CONSEQUENCES

A⁺

A⁺

THINGS TO GET DONE TODAY:

_____
_____
_____
_____
_____
_____
_____
_____
_____

TODAY'S APPOINTMENT:

TIME:	EVENT:

A⁺

FOR TOMORROW:

_____
_____
_____
_____
_____

		1	2	3	4	5	6	7	8	9	10
IMPULSIVITY	Easily Frustrated	1	2	3	4	5	6	7	8	9	10
	Acting Without Thikining	1	2	3	4	5	6	7	8	9	10
	Interrupting Others	1	2	3	4	5	6	7	8	9	10
	Emotional Outbursts	1	2	3	4	5	6	7	8	9	10
HYPERACTIVITY	Difficulty Sleeping	1	2	3	4	5	6	7	8	9	10
	Constantly Moving	1	2	3	4	5	6	7	8	9	10
	Unable to Sit Still / Fidgeting	1	2	3	4	5	6	7	8	9	10
	Excessive Talking	1	2	3	4	5	6	7	8	9	10
INATTENTION	Easily Distracted	1	2	3	4	5	6	7	8	9	10
	Careless Mistakes	1	2	3	4	5	6	7	8	9	10
	Short Attention	1	2	3	4	5	6	7	8	9	10
	Forgetfulness	1	2	3	4	5	6	7	8	9	10

DAILY PLANNER

Today's goals

Mood:

Water Intake:

Priorities with Consequences

A⁺

A⁺

A⁺

Things to get done today:

_____
_____
_____
_____
_____
_____
_____
_____
_____

Today's appointment:

TIME:	EVENT:

For tomorrow:

_____
_____
_____
_____
_____

		1	2	3	4	5	6	7	8	9	10
IMPULSIVITY	Easily Frustrated	1	2	3	4	5	6	7	8	9	10
	Acting Without Thikining	1	2	3	4	5	6	7	8	9	10
	Interrupting Others	1	2	3	4	5	6	7	8	9	10
	Emotional Outbursts	1	2	3	4	5	6	7	8	9	10
HYPERACTIVITY	Difficulty Sleeping	1	2	3	4	5	6	7	8	9	10
	Constantly Moving	1	2	3	4	5	6	7	8	9	10
	Unable to Sit Still / Fidgeting	1	2	3	4	5	6	7	8	9	10
	Excessive Talking	1	2	3	4	5	6	7	8	9	10
INATTENTION	Easily Distracted	1	2	3	4	5	6	7	8	9	10
	Careless Mistakes	1	2	3	4	5	6	7	8	9	10
	Short Attention	1	2	3	4	5	6	7	8	9	10
	Forgetfulness	1	2	3	4	5	6	7	8	9	10

 *Date* _____

DAILY PLANNER

Today's goals

Mood:

Water Intake:

Priorities with Consequences

A⁺

A⁺

A⁺

Things to get done today:

_____
_____
_____
_____
_____
_____
_____
_____

Today's appointment:

TIME:	EVENT:

For tomorrow:

_____
_____
_____
_____
_____

		1	2	3	4	5	6	7	8	9	10
IMPULSIVITY	Easily Frustrated	1	2	3	4	5	6	7	8	9	10
	Acting Without Thikining	1	2	3	4	5	6	7	8	9	10
	Interrupting Others	1	2	3	4	5	6	7	8	9	10
	Emotional Outbursts	1	2	3	4	5	6	7	8	9	10
HYPERACTIVITY	Difficulty Sleeping	1	2	3	4	5	6	7	8	9	10
	Constantly Moving	1	2	3	4	5	6	7	8	9	10
	Unable to Sit Still / Fidgeting	1	2	3	4	5	6	7	8	9	10
	Excessive Talking	1	2	3	4	5	6	7	8	9	10
INATTENTION	Easily Distracted	1	2	3	4	5	6	7	8	9	10
	Careless Mistakes	1	2	3	4	5	6	7	8	9	10
	Short Attention	1	2	3	4	5	6	7	8	9	10
	Forgetfulness	1	2	3	4	5	6	7	8	9	10

DAILY PLANNER

TODAY'S GOALS

MOOD:

PRIORITIES WITH CONSEQUENCES

WATER INTAKE:

THINGS TO GET DONE TODAY:

_____
_____
_____
_____
_____
_____
_____
_____

TODAY'S APPOINTMENT:

TIME: EVENT:

FOR TOMORROW:

_____
_____
_____
_____
_____
_____

		1	2	3	4	5	6	7	8	9	10
IMPULSIVITY	Easily Frustrated	1	2	3	4	5	6	7	8	9	10
	Acting Without Thikining	1	2	3	4	5	6	7	8	9	10
	Interrupting Others	1	2	3	4	5	6	7	8	9	10
	Emotional Outbursts	1	2	3	4	5	6	7	8	9	10
HYPERACTIVITY	Difficulty Sleeping	1	2	3	4	5	6	7	8	9	10
	Constantly Moving	1	2	3	4	5	6	7	8	9	10
	Unable to Sit Still / Fidgeting	1	2	3	4	5	6	7	8	9	10
	Excessive Talking	1	2	3	4	5	6	7	8	9	10
INATTENTION	Easily Distracted	1	2	3	4	5	6	7	8	9	10
	Careless Mistakes	1	2	3	4	5	6	7	8	9	10
	Short Attention	1	2	3	4	5	6	7	8	9	10
	Forgetfulness	1	2	3	4	5	6	7	8	9	10

Date _____

DAILY PLANNER

Today's goals

Mood:

Water Intake:

Priorities with Consequences

| A⁺ |

| A⁺ |

Things to get done today:

_____
_____
_____
_____
_____
_____
_____
_____
_____

Today's appointment:

TIME:	EVENT:

| A⁺ |

For tomorrow:

_____
_____
_____
_____
_____
_____

		1	2	3	4	5	6	7	8	9	10
IMPULSIVITY	Easily Frustrated	1	2	3	4	5	6	7	8	9	10
	Acting Without Thikining	1	2	3	4	5	6	7	8	9	10
	Interrupting Others	1	2	3	4	5	6	7	8	9	10
	Emotional Outbursts	1	2	3	4	5	6	7	8	9	10
HYPERACTIVITY	Difficulty Sleeping	1	2	3	4	5	6	7	8	9	10
	Constantly Moving	1	2	3	4	5	6	7	8	9	10
	Unable to Sit Still / Fidgeting	1	2	3	4	5	6	7	8	9	10
	Excessive Talking	1	2	3	4	5	6	7	8	9	10
INATTENTION	Easily Distracted	1	2	3	4	5	6	7	8	9	10
	Careless Mistakes	1	2	3	4	5	6	7	8	9	10
	Short Attention	1	2	3	4	5	6	7	8	9	10
	Forgetfulness	1	2	3	4	5	6	7	8	9	10

MEDICATION
Tracker

	MEDICATION	DOSAGE	FREQUENCY	TAKEN
MONDAY				
TUESDAY				
WEDNESDAY				
THURSDAY				
FRIDAY				
SATURDAY				
SUNDAY				

NOTES

Nothing like ADHD and a good
fight to the death to make time fly.

—RICK RIORDAN

TO DO'S
Weekly

MUST DO!

_____
_____
_____

IMPORTANT

- _____
- _____
- _____
- _____
- _____
- _____
- _____
- _____
- _____
- _____

LESS IMPORTANT

- _____
- _____
- _____
- _____
- _____
- _____
- _____
- _____
- _____
- _____

NOTES

_____   _____
_____   _____
_____   _____
_____   _____

*In the power of fixing the attention lies the
most precious of the intellectual habits.*
– ROBERT HALL

HABIT TRACKER
Weekly

HÁBITS	MON	TUES	WED	THU	FRI	SAT	SUN
	○	○	○	○	○	○	○
	○	○	○	○	○	○	○
	○	○	○	○	○	○	○
	○	○	○	○	○	○	○
	○	○	○	○	○	○	○
	○	○	○	○	○	○	○
	○	○	○	○	○	○	○
	○	○	○	○	○	○	○
	○	○	○	○	○	○	○
	○	○	○	○	○	○	○
	○	○	○	○	○	○	○
	○	○	○	○	○	○	○
	○	○	○	○	○	○	○
	○	○	○	○	○	○	○

HOW DID I DO?

"I have more thoughts before breakfast
than most people have all day."
— UNKNOWN

BRAIN DUMP

Though Organizer

MUST DO	SHOULD DO
COULD START	**MUST DO**

Date _____

DAILY PLANNER

TODAY'S GOALS

MOOD:

😄 🙂 😐 🙁 😞

WATER INTAKE:

⬭ ⬭ ⬭ ⬭ ⬭ ⬭ ⬭ ⬭

PRIORITIES WITH CONSEQUENCES

A⁺

A⁺

A⁺

THINGS TO GET DONE TODAY:

_____
_____
_____
_____
_____
_____
_____
_____
_____
_____

TODAY'S APPOINTMENT:

TIME:	EVENT:

FOR TOMORROW:

_____
_____
_____
_____
_____
_____

		1	2	3	4	5	6	7	8	9	10
IMPULSIVITY	Easily Frustrated	1	2	3	4	5	6	7	8	9	10
	Acting Without Thikinking	1	2	3	4	5	6	7	8	9	10
	Interrupting Others	1	2	3	4	5	6	7	8	9	10
	Emotional Outbursts	1	2	3	4	5	6	7	8	9	10
HYPERACTIVITY	Difficulty Sleeping	1	2	3	4	5	6	7	8	9	10
	Constantly Moving	1	2	3	4	5	6	7	8	9	10
	Unable to Sit Still / Fidgeting	1	2	3	4	5	6	7	8	9	10
	Excessive Talking	1	2	3	4	5	6	7	8	9	10
INATTENTION	Easily Distracted	1	2	3	4	5	6	7	8	9	10
	Careless Mistakes	1	2	3	4	5	6	7	8	9	10
	Short Attention	1	2	3	4	5	6	7	8	9	10
	Forgetfulness	1	2	3	4	5	6	7	8	9	10

Date _____

DAILY PLANNER

Today's Goals

Mood:
🙂 🙂 😐 🙁 😢

Water Intake:
◇ ◇ ◇ ◇ ◇ ◇ ◇ ◇

Priorities with Consequences

A⁺

A⁺

A⁺

Things to get done today:

_____
_____
_____
_____
_____
_____
_____
_____

Today's Appointment:

Time:	Event:

For tomorrow:

_____
_____
_____
_____
_____

Category	Symptom	Rating
Impulsivity	Easily Frustrated	1 2 3 4 5 6 7 8 9 10
	Acting Without Thikining	1 2 3 4 5 6 7 8 9 10
	Interrupting Others	1 2 3 4 5 6 7 8 9 10
	Emotional Outbursts	1 2 3 4 5 6 7 8 9 10
Hyperactivity	Difficulty Sleeping	1 2 3 4 5 6 7 8 9 10
	Constantly Moving	1 2 3 4 5 6 7 8 9 10
	Unable to Sit Still / Fidgeting	1 2 3 4 5 6 7 8 9 10
	Excessive Talking	1 2 3 4 5 6 7 8 9 10
Inattention	Easily Distracted	1 2 3 4 5 6 7 8 9 10
	Careless Mistakes	1 2 3 4 5 6 7 8 9 10
	Short Attention	1 2 3 4 5 6 7 8 9 10
	Forgetfulness	1 2 3 4 5 6 7 8 9 10

Date _____

DAILY PLANNER

Today's goals

Mood:

😊 🙂 😐 🙁 😢

Water Intake:

💧 💧 💧 💧 💧 💧 💧 💧

Priorities with Consequences

A⁺

A⁺

A⁺

Things to get done today:

_____
_____
_____
_____
_____
_____
_____
_____

Today's appointment:

TIME:	EVENT:

For tomorrow:

_____
_____
_____
_____
_____

		1	2	3	4	5	6	7	8	9	10
IMPULSIVITY	Easily Frustrated	1	2	3	4	5	6	7	8	9	10
	Acting Without Thikining	1	2	3	4	5	6	7	8	9	10
	Interrupting Others	1	2	3	4	5	6	7	8	9	10
	Emotional Outbursts	1	2	3	4	5	6	7	8	9	10
HYPERACTIVITY	Difficulty Sleeping	1	2	3	4	5	6	7	8	9	10
	Constantly Moving	1	2	3	4	5	6	7	8	9	10
	Unable to Sit Still / Fidgeting	1	2	3	4	5	6	7	8	9	10
	Excessive Talking	1	2	3	4	5	6	7	8	9	10
INATTENTION	Easily Distracted	1	2	3	4	5	6	7	8	9	10
	Careless Mistakes	1	2	3	4	5	6	7	8	9	10
	Short Attention	1	2	3	4	5	6	7	8	9	10
	Forgetfulness	1	2	3	4	5	6	7	8	9	10

DAILY PLANNER

TODAY'S GOALS

MOOD:

WATER INTAKE:

PRIORITIES WITH CONSEQUENCES

A⁺

A⁺

THINGS TO GET DONE TODAY:

_____
_____
_____
_____
_____
_____
_____
_____
_____

TODAY'S APPOINTMENT:

TIME:	EVENT:

A⁺

FOR TOMORROW:

_____
_____
_____
_____
_____

		1	2	3	4	5	6	7	8	9	10
IMPULSIVITY	Easily Frustrated	1	2	3	4	5	6	7	8	9	10
	Acting Without Thikining	1	2	3	4	5	6	7	8	9	10
	Interrupting Others	1	2	3	4	5	6	7	8	9	10
	Emotional Outbursts	1	2	3	4	5	6	7	8	9	10
HYPERACTIVITY	Difficulty Sleeping	1	2	3	4	5	6	7	8	9	10
	Constantly Moving	1	2	3	4	5	6	7	8	9	10
	Unable to Sit Still / Fidgeting	1	2	3	4	5	6	7	8	9	10
	Excessive Talking	1	2	3	4	5	6	7	8	9	10
INATTENTION	Easily Distracted	1	2	3	4	5	6	7	8	9	10
	Careless Mistakes	1	2	3	4	5	6	7	8	9	10
	Short Attention	1	2	3	4	5	6	7	8	9	10
	Forgetfulness	1	2	3	4	5	6	7	8	9	10

Date _____

DAILY PLANNER

Today's goals

Mood:

Water Intake:

Priorities with Consequences

A⁺

A⁺

A⁺

Things to get done today:

_____
_____
_____
_____
_____
_____
_____
_____

Today's appointment:

TIME:	EVENT:

For tomorrow:

_____
_____
_____
_____
_____

		1	2	3	4	5	6	7	8	9	10
IMPULSIVITY	Easily Frustrated	1	2	3	4	5	6	7	8	9	10
	Acting Without Thikining	1	2	3	4	5	6	7	8	9	10
	Interrupting Others	1	2	3	4	5	6	7	8	9	10
	Emotional Outbursts	1	2	3	4	5	6	7	8	9	10
HYPERACTIVITY	Difficulty Sleeping	1	2	3	4	5	6	7	8	9	10
	Constantly Moving	1	2	3	4	5	6	7	8	9	10
	Unable to Sit Still / Fidgeting	1	2	3	4	5	6	7	8	9	10
	Excessive Talking	1	2	3	4	5	6	7	8	9	10
INATTENTION	Easily Distracted	1	2	3	4	5	6	7	8	9	10
	Careless Mistakes	1	2	3	4	5	6	7	8	9	10
	Short Attention	1	2	3	4	5	6	7	8	9	10
	Forgetfulness	1	2	3	4	5	6	7	8	9	10

Date _____

DAILY PLANNER

TODAY'S GOALS

MOOD:

WATER INTAKE:

PRIORITIES WITH CONSEQUENCES

A⁺

A⁺

A⁺

THINGS TO GET DONE TODAY:

_____
_____
_____
_____
_____
_____
_____
_____
_____

TODAY'S APPOINTMENT:

TIME:	EVENT:

FOR TOMORROW:

_____
_____
_____
_____
_____

		1	2	3	4	5	6	7	8	9	10
IMPULSIVITY	Easily Frustrated	1	2	3	4	5	6	7	8	9	10
	Acting Without Thikining	1	2	3	4	5	6	7	8	9	10
	Interrupting Others	1	2	3	4	5	6	7	8	9	10
	Emotional Outbursts	1	2	3	4	5	6	7	8	9	10
HYPERACTIVITY	Difficulty Sleeping	1	2	3	4	5	6	7	8	9	10
	Constantly Moving	1	2	3	4	5	6	7	8	9	10
	Unable to Sit Still / Fidgeting	1	2	3	4	5	6	7	8	9	10
	Excessive Talking	1	2	3	4	5	6	7	8	9	10
INATTENTION	Easily Distracted	1	2	3	4	5	6	7	8	9	10
	Careless Mistakes	1	2	3	4	5	6	7	8	9	10
	Short Attention	1	2	3	4	5	6	7	8	9	10
	Forgetfulness	1	2	3	4	5	6	7	8	9	10

 $\mathcal{D}ate$ _____

DAILY PLANNER

Today's goals

Mood:

☺ ☺ ☺ ☹ ☹

Water Intake:

◊ ◊ ◊ ◊ ◊ ◊ ◊ ◊

Priorities with Consequences

A⁺

A⁺

A⁺

Things to get done today:

_____
_____
_____
_____
_____
_____
_____
_____
_____

Today's appointment:

TIME:	EVENT:

For tomorrow:

_____
_____
_____
_____
_____

		1	2	3	4	5	6	7	8	9	10
IMPULSIVITY	Easily Frustrated	1	2	3	4	5	6	7	8	9	10
	Acting Without Thikining	1	2	3	4	5	6	7	8	9	10
	Interrupting Others	1	2	3	4	5	6	7	8	9	10
	Emotional Outbursts	1	2	3	4	5	6	7	8	9	10
HYPERACTIVITY	Difficulty Sleeping	1	2	3	4	5	6	7	8	9	10
	Constantly Moving	1	2	3	4	5	6	7	8	9	10
	Unable to Sit Still / Fidgeting	1	2	3	4	5	6	7	8	9	10
	Excessive Talking	1	2	3	4	5	6	7	8	9	10
INATTENTION	Easily Distracted	1	2	3	4	5	6	7	8	9	10
	Careless Mistakes	1	2	3	4	5	6	7	8	9	10
	Short Attention	1	2	3	4	5	6	7	8	9	10
	Forgetfulness	1	2	3	4	5	6	7	8	9	10

MEDICATION
Tracker

	MEDICATION	DOSAGE	FREQUENCY	TAKEN
MONDAY				
TUESDAY				
WEDNESDAY				
THURSDAY				
FRIDAY				
SATURDAY				
SUNDAY				

NOTES

Nothing like ADHD and a good
fight to the death to make time fly.

—RICK RIORDAN

TO DO'S
Weekly

MUST DO!

_____

_____

_____

IMPORTANT

- _____
- _____
- _____
- _____
- _____
- _____
- _____
- _____
- _____
- _____

LESS IMPORTANT

- _____
- _____
- _____
- _____
- _____
- _____
- _____
- _____
- _____
- _____

NOTES

_____   _____

_____   _____

_____   _____

HABIT TRACKER
Weekly

HÁBITS	MON	TUES	WED	THU	FRI	SAT	SUN
	○	○	○	○	○	○	○
	○	○	○	○	○	○	○
	○	○	○	○	○	○	○
	○	○	○	○	○	○	○
	○	○	○	○	○	○	○
	○	○	○	○	○	○	○
	○	○	○	○	○	○	○
	○	○	○	○	○	○	○
	○	○	○	○	○	○	○
	○	○	○	○	○	○	○
	○	○	○	○	○	○	○
	○	○	○	○	○	○	○
	○	○	○	○	○	○	○
	○	○	○	○	○	○	○
	○	○	○	○	○	○	○

HOW DID I DO?

*"I have more thoughts before breakfast
than most people have all day."*
— UNKNOWN

BRAIN DUMP
Though Organizer

MUST DO	SHOULD DO
COULD START	MUST DO

DAILY PLANNER

TODAY'S GOALS

MOOD:

WATER INTAKE:

PRIORITIES WITH CONSEQUENCES

A⁺

A⁺

THINGS TO GET DONE TODAY:

TODAY'S APPOINTMENT:

A⁺

TIME:	EVENT:

FOR TOMORROW:

		1	2	3	4	5	6	7	8	9	10
IMPULSIVITY	Easily Frustrated	1	2	3	4	5	6	7	8	9	10
	Acting Without Thikining	1	2	3	4	5	6	7	8	9	10
	Interrupting Others	1	2	3	4	5	6	7	8	9	10
	Emotional Outbursts	1	2	3	4	5	6	7	8	9	10
HYPERACTIVITY	Difficulty Sleeping	1	2	3	4	5	6	7	8	9	10
	Constantly Moving	1	2	3	4	5	6	7	8	9	10
	Unable to Sit Still / Fidgeting	1	2	3	4	5	6	7	8	9	10
	Excessive Talking	1	2	3	4	5	6	7	8	9	10
INATTENTION	Easily Distracted	1	2	3	4	5	6	7	8	9	10
	Careless Mistakes	1	2	3	4	5	6	7	8	9	10
	Short Attention	1	2	3	4	5	6	7	8	9	10
	Forgetfulness	1	2	3	4	5	6	7	8	9	10

Date _____

DAILY PLANNER

TODAY'S GOALS

MOOD:

😊 🙂 😐 😕 ☹️

WATER INTAKE:

◇ ◇ ◇ ◇ ◇ ◇ ◇ ◇

PRIORITIES WITH CONSEQUENCES

[A⁺]

[A⁺]

[A⁺]

THINGS TO GET DONE TODAY:

_____
_____
_____
_____
_____
_____
_____
_____

TODAY'S APPOINTMENT:

TIME:	EVENT:

FOR TOMORROW:

_____
_____
_____
_____
_____

		1	2	3	4	5	6	7	8	9	10
IMPULSIVITY	Easily Frustrated	1	2	3	4	5	6	7	8	9	10
	Acting Without Thikining	1	2	3	4	5	6	7	8	9	10
	Interrupting Others	1	2	3	4	5	6	7	8	9	10
	Emotional Outbursts	1	2	3	4	5	6	7	8	9	10
HYPERACTIVITY	Difficulty Sleeping	1	2	3	4	5	6	7	8	9	10
	Constantly Moving	1	2	3	4	5	6	7	8	9	10
	Unable to Sit Still / Fidgeting	1	2	3	4	5	6	7	8	9	10
	Excessive Talking	1	2	3	4	5	6	7	8	9	10
INATTENTION	Easily Distracted	1	2	3	4	5	6	7	8	9	10
	Careless Mistakes	1	2	3	4	5	6	7	8	9	10
	Short Attention	1	2	3	4	5	6	7	8	9	10
	Forgetfulness	1	2	3	4	5	6	7	8	9	10

DAILY PLANNER

Today's goals

Mood:

Water Intake:

Priorities with Consequences

A⁺

A⁺

A⁺

Things to get done today:

_____

_____

_____

_____

_____

_____

_____

_____

Today's appointment:

TIME:	EVENT:

For tomorrow:

_____

_____

_____

_____

_____

		1	2	3	4	5	6	7	8	9	10
IMPULSIVITY	Easily Frustrated	1	2	3	4	5	6	7	8	9	10
	Acting Without Thikining	1	2	3	4	5	6	7	8	9	10
	Interrupting Others	1	2	3	4	5	6	7	8	9	10
	Emotional Outbursts	1	2	3	4	5	6	7	8	9	10
HYPERACTIVITY	Difficulty Sleeping	1	2	3	4	5	6	7	8	9	10
	Constantly Moving	1	2	3	4	5	6	7	8	9	10
	Unable to Sit Still / Fidgeting	1	2	3	4	5	6	7	8	9	10
	Excessive Talking	1	2	3	4	5	6	7	8	9	10
INATTENTION	Easily Distracted	1	2	3	4	5	6	7	8	9	10
	Careless Mistakes	1	2	3	4	5	6	7	8	9	10
	Short Attention	1	2	3	4	5	6	7	8	9	10
	Forgetfulness	1	2	3	4	5	6	7	8	9	10

DAILY PLANNER

Today's goals

Mood:

Water Intake:

Priorities with Consequences

Things to get done today:

_____
_____
_____
_____
_____
_____
_____
_____
_____

Today's appointment:

TIME:	EVENT:

For tomorrow:

_____
_____
_____
_____
_____

		1	2	3	4	5	6	7	8	9	10
IMPULSIVITY	Easily Frustrated	1	2	3	4	5	6	7	8	9	10
	Acting Without Thikining	1	2	3	4	5	6	7	8	9	10
	Interrupting Others	1	2	3	4	5	6	7	8	9	10
	Emotional Outbursts	1	2	3	4	5	6	7	8	9	10
HYPERACTIVITY	Difficulty Sleeping	1	2	3	4	5	6	7	8	9	10
	Constantly Moving	1	2	3	4	5	6	7	8	9	10
	Unable to Sit Still / Fidgeting	1	2	3	4	5	6	7	8	9	10
	Excessive Talking	1	2	3	4	5	6	7	8	9	10
INATTENTION	Easily Distracted	1	2	3	4	5	6	7	8	9	10
	Careless Mistakes	1	2	3	4	5	6	7	8	9	10
	Short Attention	1	2	3	4	5	6	7	8	9	10
	Forgetfulness	1	2	3	4	5	6	7	8	9	10

Date _____

DAILY PLANNER

Today's goals

Mood:

😊 🙂 😐 🙁 😢

Water Intake:

💧 💧 💧 💧 💧 💧 💧 💧

Priorities with Consequences

[A⁺]

[A⁺]

[A⁺]

Things to get done today:

_____
_____
_____
_____
_____
_____
_____
_____

Today's appointment:

TIME:	EVENT:

For tomorrow:

_____
_____
_____
_____
_____

		1	2	3	4	5	6	7	8	9	10
IMPULSIVITY	Easily Frustrated	1	2	3	4	5	6	7	8	9	10
	Acting Without Thikining	1	2	3	4	5	6	7	8	9	10
	Interrupting Others	1	2	3	4	5	6	7	8	9	10
	Emotional Outbursts	1	2	3	4	5	6	7	8	9	10
HYPERACTIVITY	Difficulty Sleeping	1	2	3	4	5	6	7	8	9	10
	Constantly Moving	1	2	3	4	5	6	7	8	9	10
	Unable to Sit Still / Fidgeting	1	2	3	4	5	6	7	8	9	10
	Excessive Talking	1	2	3	4	5	6	7	8	9	10
INATTENTION	Easily Distracted	1	2	3	4	5	6	7	8	9	10
	Careless Mistakes	1	2	3	4	5	6	7	8	9	10
	Short Attention	1	2	3	4	5	6	7	8	9	10
	Forgetfulness	1	2	3	4	5	6	7	8	9	10

Date _____

DAILY PLANNER

TODAY'S GOALS

MOOD:

WATER INTAKE:

PRIORITIES WITH CONSEQUENCES

A⁺

A⁺

A⁺

THINGS TO GET DONE TODAY:
_____
_____
_____
_____
_____
_____
_____
_____

TODAY'S APPOINTMENT:

TIME:	EVENT:

FOR TOMORROW:
_____
_____
_____
_____
_____

		1	2	3	4	5	6	7	8	9	10
IMPULSIVITY	Easily Frustrated	1	2	3	4	5	6	7	8	9	10
	Acting Without Thiking	1	2	3	4	5	6	7	8	9	10
	Interrupting Others	1	2	3	4	5	6	7	8	9	10
	Emotional Outbursts	1	2	3	4	5	6	7	8	9	10
HYPERACTIVITY	Difficulty Sleeping	1	2	3	4	5	6	7	8	9	10
	Constantly Moving	1	2	3	4	5	6	7	8	9	10
	Unable to Sit Still / Fidgeting	1	2	3	4	5	6	7	8	9	10
	Excessive Talking	1	2	3	4	5	6	7	8	9	10
INATTENTION	Easily Distracted	1	2	3	4	5	6	7	8	9	10
	Careless Mistakes	1	2	3	4	5	6	7	8	9	10
	Short Attention	1	2	3	4	5	6	7	8	9	10
	Forgetfulness	1	2	3	4	5	6	7	8	9	10

DAILY PLANNER

TODAY'S GOALS

MOOD:

WATER INTAKE:

PRIORITIES WITH CONSEQUENCES

A⁺

A⁺

A⁺

THINGS TO GET DONE TODAY:

_____
_____
_____
_____
_____
_____
_____
_____
_____

TODAY'S APPOINTMENT:

TIME:	EVENT:

FOR TOMORROW:

_____
_____
_____
_____
_____

		1	2	3	4	5	6	7	8	9	10
IMPULSIVITY	Easily Frustrated	1	2	3	4	5	6	7	8	9	10
	Acting Without Thikining	1	2	3	4	5	6	7	8	9	10
	Interrupting Others	1	2	3	4	5	6	7	8	9	10
	Emotional Outbursts	1	2	3	4	5	6	7	8	9	10
HYPERACTIVITY	Difficulty Sleeping	1	2	3	4	5	6	7	8	9	10
	Constantly Moving	1	2	3	4	5	6	7	8	9	10
	Unable to Sit Still / Fidgeting	1	2	3	4	5	6	7	8	9	10
	Excessive Talking	1	2	3	4	5	6	7	8	9	10
INATTENTION	Easily Distracted	1	2	3	4	5	6	7	8	9	10
	Careless Mistakes	1	2	3	4	5	6	7	8	9	10
	Short Attention	1	2	3	4	5	6	7	8	9	10
	Forgetfulness	1	2	3	4	5	6	7	8	9	10

MEDICATION
Tracker

	MEDICATION	DOSAGE	FREQUENCY	TAKEN
MONDAY				
TUESDAY				
WEDNESDAY				
THURSDAY				
FRIDAY				
SATURDAY				
SUNDAY				

NOTES

Nothing like ADHD and a good
fight to the death to make time fly.

—Rick Riordan

TO DO'S
Weekly

Must Do!

_____
_____
_____

Important

- _____
- _____
- _____
- _____
- _____
- _____
- _____
- _____
- _____
- _____

Less important

- _____
- _____
- _____
- _____
- _____
- _____
- _____
- _____
- _____
- _____

Notes

_____   _____
_____   _____
_____   _____
_____   _____

In the power of fixing the attention lies the most precious of the intellectual habits.
– Robert Hall

HABIT TRACKER
Weekly

HÁBITS	MON	TUES	WED	THU	FRI	SAT	SUN
_____	◯	◯	◯	◯	◯	◯	◯
_____	◯	◯	◯	◯	◯	◯	◯
_____	◯	◯	◯	◯	◯	◯	◯
_____	◯	◯	◯	◯	◯	◯	◯
_____	◯	◯	◯	◯	◯	◯	◯
_____	◯	◯	◯	◯	◯	◯	◯
_____	◯	◯	◯	◯	◯	◯	◯
_____	◯	◯	◯	◯	◯	◯	◯
_____	◯	◯	◯	◯	◯	◯	◯
_____	◯	◯	◯	◯	◯	◯	◯
_____	◯	◯	◯	◯	◯	◯	◯
_____	◯	◯	◯	◯	◯	◯	◯
_____	◯	◯	◯	◯	◯	◯	◯
_____	◯	◯	◯	◯	◯	◯	◯

HOW DID I DO?

"I have more thoughts before breakfast
than most people have all day."
— UNKNOWN

BRAIN DUMP

Though Organizer

MUST DO	SHOULD DO
COULD START	**MUST DO**

 Date _____

DAILY PLANNER

Today's goals

Mood:

Priorities with Consequences

Water Intake:

Things to get done today:

_____
_____
_____
_____
_____
_____
_____
_____
_____

Today's appointment:

TIME:	EVENT:

For tomorrow:

_____
_____
_____
_____
_____
_____

		1	2	3	4	5	6	7	8	9	10
IMPULSIVITY	Easily Frustrated	1	2	3	4	5	6	7	8	9	10
	Acting Without Thikining	1	2	3	4	5	6	7	8	9	10
	Interrupting Others	1	2	3	4	5	6	7	8	9	10
	Emotional Outbursts	1	2	3	4	5	6	7	8	9	10
HYPERACTIVITY	Difficulty Sleeping	1	2	3	4	5	6	7	8	9	10
	Constantly Moving	1	2	3	4	5	6	7	8	9	10
	Unable to Sit Still / Fidgeting	1	2	3	4	5	6	7	8	9	10
	Excessive Talking	1	2	3	4	5	6	7	8	9	10
INATTENTION	Easily Distracted	1	2	3	4	5	6	7	8	9	10
	Careless Mistakes	1	2	3	4	5	6	7	8	9	10
	Short Attention	1	2	3	4	5	6	7	8	9	10
	Forgetfulness	1	2	3	4	5	6	7	8	9	10

Date _____

DAILY PLANNER

TODAY'S GOALS

MOOD:

PRIORITIES WITH CONSEQUENCES

A

WATER INTAKE:

A

THINGS TO GET DONE TODAY:

_____
_____
_____
_____
_____
_____
_____
_____

TODAY'S APPOINTMENT:

TIME:	EVENT:

A

FOR TOMORROW:

_____
_____
_____
_____
_____
_____

		1	2	3	4	5	6	7	8	9	10
IMPULSIVITY	Easily Frustrated	1	2	3	4	5	6	7	8	9	10
	Acting Without Thikining	1	2	3	4	5	6	7	8	9	10
	Interrupting Others	1	2	3	4	5	6	7	8	9	10
	Emotional Outbursts	1	2	3	4	5	6	7	8	9	10
HYPERACTIVITY	Difficulty Sleeping	1	2	3	4	5	6	7	8	9	10
	Constantly Moving	1	2	3	4	5	6	7	8	9	10
	Unable to Sit Still / Fidgeting	1	2	3	4	5	6	7	8	9	10
	Excessive Talking	1	2	3	4	5	6	7	8	9	10
INATTENTION	Easily Distracted	1	2	3	4	5	6	7	8	9	10
	Careless Mistakes	1	2	3	4	5	6	7	8	9	10
	Short Attention	1	2	3	4	5	6	7	8	9	10
	Forgetfulness	1	2	3	4	5	6	7	8	9	10

 *Date* _____

DAILY PLANNER

Today's Goals

Mood:

Priorities with Consequences

A⁺

Water Intake:

A⁺

Things to get done today:

_____
_____
_____
_____
_____
_____
_____
_____

Today's appointment:

A⁺

TIME:	EVENT:

For tomorrow:

_____
_____
_____
_____
_____
_____

		1	2	3	4	5	6	7	8	9	10
IMPULSIVITY	Easily Frustrated	1	2	3	4	5	6	7	8	9	10
	Acting Without Thikining	1	2	3	4	5	6	7	8	9	10
	Interrupting Others	1	2	3	4	5	6	7	8	9	10
	Emotional Outbursts	1	2	3	4	5	6	7	8	9	10
HYPERACTIVITY	Difficulty Sleeping	1	2	3	4	5	6	7	8	9	10
	Constantly Moving	1	2	3	4	5	6	7	8	9	10
	Unable to Sit Still / Fidgeting	1	2	3	4	5	6	7	8	9	10
	Excessive Talking	1	2	3	4	5	6	7	8	9	10
INATTENTION	Easily Distracted	1	2	3	4	5	6	7	8	9	10
	Careless Mistakes	1	2	3	4	5	6	7	8	9	10
	Short Attention	1	2	3	4	5	6	7	8	9	10
	Forgetfulness	1	2	3	4	5	6	7	8	9	10

Date _____

DAILY PLANNER

TODAY'S GOALS

MOOD:

WATER INTAKE:

PRIORITIES WITH CONSEQUENCES

THINGS TO GET DONE TODAY:

TODAY'S APPOINTMENT:

TIME: EVENT:

FOR TOMORROW:

		1	2	3	4	5	6	7	8	9	10
IMPULSIVITY	Easily Frustrated	1	2	3	4	5	6	7	8	9	10
	Acting Without Thikining	1	2	3	4	5	6	7	8	9	10
	Interrupting Others	1	2	3	4	5	6	7	8	9	10
	Emotional Outbursts	1	2	3	4	5	6	7	8	9	10
HYPERACTIVITY	Difficulty Sleeping	1	2	3	4	5	6	7	8	9	10
	Constantly Moving	1	2	3	4	5	6	7	8	9	10
	Unable to Sit Still / Fidgeting	1	2	3	4	5	6	7	8	9	10
	Excessive Talking	1	2	3	4	5	6	7	8	9	10
INATTENTION	Easily Distracted	1	2	3	4	5	6	7	8	9	10
	Careless Mistakes	1	2	3	4	5	6	7	8	9	10
	Short Attention	1	2	3	4	5	6	7	8	9	10
	Forgetfulness	1	2	3	4	5	6	7	8	9	10

DAILY PLANNER

TODAY'S GOALS

MOOD:

😄 🙂 😐 🙁 😞

WATER INTAKE:

💧💧💧💧💧💧💧💧

PRIORITIES WITH CONSEQUENCES

A⁺

A⁺

THINGS TO GET DONE TODAY:

_____
_____
_____
_____
_____
_____
_____
_____
_____

TODAY'S APPOINTMENT:

TIME:	EVENT:

A⁺

FOR TOMORROW:

_____
_____
_____
_____
_____

		1	2	3	4	5	6	7	8	9	10
IMPULSIVITY	Easily Frustrated	1	2	3	4	5	6	7	8	9	10
	Acting Without Thikining	1	2	3	4	5	6	7	8	9	10
	Interrupting Others	1	2	3	4	5	6	7	8	9	10
	Emotional Outbursts	1	2	3	4	5	6	7	8	9	10
HYPERACTIVITY	Difficulty Sleeping	1	2	3	4	5	6	7	8	9	10
	Constantly Moving	1	2	3	4	5	6	7	8	9	10
	Unable to Sit Still / Fidgeting	1	2	3	4	5	6	7	8	9	10
	Excessive Talking	1	2	3	4	5	6	7	8	9	10
INATTENTION	Easily Distracted	1	2	3	4	5	6	7	8	9	10
	Careless Mistakes	1	2	3	4	5	6	7	8	9	10
	Short Attention	1	2	3	4	5	6	7	8	9	10
	Forgetfulness	1	2	3	4	5	6	7	8	9	10

Date _____

DAILY PLANNER

🎯 Today's Goals

Mood:
😏 🙂 😐 🙁 😢

Water Intake:
💧 💧 💧 💧 💧 💧 💧 💧

Priorities with Consequences

A⁺

A⁺

A⁺

Things to get done today:
_____
_____
_____
_____
_____
_____
_____
_____
_____

Today's appointment:

Time:	Event:

For tomorrow:
_____
_____
_____
_____

		1	2	3	4	5	6	7	8	9	10
IMPULSIVITY	Easily Frustrated	1	2	3	4	5	6	7	8	9	10
	Acting Without Thikining	1	2	3	4	5	6	7	8	9	10
	Interrupting Others	1	2	3	4	5	6	7	8	9	10
	Emotional Outbursts	1	2	3	4	5	6	7	8	9	10
HYPERACTIVITY	Difficulty Sleeping	1	2	3	4	5	6	7	8	9	10
	Constantly Moving	1	2	3	4	5	6	7	8	9	10
	Unable to Sit Still / Fidgeting	1	2	3	4	5	6	7	8	9	10
	Excessive Talking	1	2	3	4	5	6	7	8	9	10
INATTENTION	Easily Distracted	1	2	3	4	5	6	7	8	9	10
	Careless Mistakes	1	2	3	4	5	6	7	8	9	10
	Short Attention	1	2	3	4	5	6	7	8	9	10
	Forgetfulness	1	2	3	4	5	6	7	8	9	10

DAILY PLANNER

TODAY'S GOALS

MOOD:

PRIORITIES WITH CONSEQUENCES

A

WATER INTAKE:

A

THINGS TO GET DONE TODAY:

TODAY'S APPOINTMENT:

A

TIME: EVENT:

FOR TOMORROW:

		1	2	3	4	5	6	7	8	9	10
IMPULSIVITY	Easily Frustrated	1	2	3	4	5	6	7	8	9	10
	Acting Without Thikining	1	2	3	4	5	6	7	8	9	10
	Interrupting Others	1	2	3	4	5	6	7	8	9	10
	Emotional Outbursts	1	2	3	4	5	6	7	8	9	10
HYPERACTIVITY	Difficulty Sleeping	1	2	3	4	5	6	7	8	9	10
	Constantly Moving	1	2	3	4	5	6	7	8	9	10
	Unable to Sit Still / Fidgeting	1	2	3	4	5	6	7	8	9	10
	Excessive Talking	1	2	3	4	5	6	7	8	9	10
INATTENTION	Easily Distracted	1	2	3	4	5	6	7	8	9	10
	Careless Mistakes	1	2	3	4	5	6	7	8	9	10
	Short Attention	1	2	3	4	5	6	7	8	9	10
	Forgetfulness	1	2	3	4	5	6	7	8	9	10

MEDICATION

Tracker

	MEDICATION	DOSAGE	FREQUENCY	TAKEN
MONDAY				
TUESDAY				
WEDNESDAY				
THURSDAY				
FRIDAY				
SATURDAY				
SUNDAY				

NOTES

Nothing like ADHD and a good
fight to the death to make time fly.

—RICK RIORDAN

TO DO'S
Weekly

MUST DO!

_____
_____
_____
_____

IMPORTANT

- _____
- _____
- _____
- _____
- _____
- _____
- _____
- _____
- _____
- _____

LESS IMPORTANT

- _____
- _____
- _____
- _____
- _____
- _____
- _____
- _____
- _____
- _____

NOTES

_____ _____
_____ _____
_____ _____
_____ _____

HABIT TRACKER
Weekly

HÁBITS	MON	TUES	WED	THU	FRI	SAT	SUN
_____	○	○	○	○	○	○	○
_____	○	○	○	○	○	○	○
_____	○	○	○	○	○	○	○
_____	○	○	○	○	○	○	○
_____	○	○	○	○	○	○	○
_____	○	○	○	○	○	○	○
_____	○	○	○	○	○	○	○
_____	○	○	○	○	○	○	○
_____	○	○	○	○	○	○	○
_____	○	○	○	○	○	○	○
_____	○	○	○	○	○	○	○
_____	○	○	○	○	○	○	○
_____	○	○	○	○	○	○	○
_____	○	○	○	○	○	○	○

HOW DID I DO?

"I have more thoughts before breakfast
than most people have all day."
— Unknown

BRAIN DUMP

Though Organizer

Must Do	Should Do
Could Start	**Must Do**

Date _____

DAILY PLANNER

Today's goals

Mood:

😄 🙂 😐 🙁 ☹️

Water Intake:

💧💧💧💧💧💧💧💧

Priorities with Consequences

A⁺

A⁺

A⁺

Things to get done today:

_____
_____
_____
_____
_____
_____
_____
_____
_____

Today's appointment:

TIME:	EVENT:

For tomorrow:

_____
_____
_____
_____
_____

		1	2	3	4	5	6	7	8	9	10
IMPULSIVITY	Easily Frustrated	1	2	3	4	5	6	7	8	9	10
	Acting Without Thikining	1	2	3	4	5	6	7	8	9	10
	Interrupting Others	1	2	3	4	5	6	7	8	9	10
	Emotional Outbursts	1	2	3	4	5	6	7	8	9	10
HYPERACTIVITY	Difficulty Sleeping	1	2	3	4	5	6	7	8	9	10
	Constantly Moving	1	2	3	4	5	6	7	8	9	10
	Unable to Sit Still / Fidgeting	1	2	3	4	5	6	7	8	9	10
	Excessive Talking	1	2	3	4	5	6	7	8	9	10
INATTENTION	Easily Distracted	1	2	3	4	5	6	7	8	9	10
	Careless Mistakes	1	2	3	4	5	6	7	8	9	10
	Short Attention	1	2	3	4	5	6	7	8	9	10
	Forgetfulness	1	2	3	4	5	6	7	8	9	10

Date _____

DAILY PLANNER

Today's goals

Mood:

😄 🙂 😐 🙁 😢

Water Intake:

△△△△△△△△

Priorities with Consequences

A⁺

A⁺

A⁺

Things to get done today:

_____
_____
_____
_____
_____
_____
_____
_____

Today's appointment:

TIME:	EVENT:

For tomorrow:

_____
_____
_____
_____
_____

		1	2	3	4	5	6	7	8	9	10
IMPULSIVITY	Easily Frustrated	1	2	3	4	5	6	7	8	9	10
	Acting Without Thikining	1	2	3	4	5	6	7	8	9	10
	Interrupting Others	1	2	3	4	5	6	7	8	9	10
	Emotional Outbursts	1	2	3	4	5	6	7	8	9	10
HYPERACTIVITY	Difficulty Sleeping	1	2	3	4	5	6	7	8	9	10
	Constantly Moving	1	2	3	4	5	6	7	8	9	10
	Unable to Sit Still / Fidgeting	1	2	3	4	5	6	7	8	9	10
	Excessive Talking	1	2	3	4	5	6	7	8	9	10
INATTENTION	Easily Distracted	1	2	3	4	5	6	7	8	9	10
	Careless Mistakes	1	2	3	4	5	6	7	8	9	10
	Short Attention	1	2	3	4	5	6	7	8	9	10
	Forgetfulness	1	2	3	4	5	6	7	8	9	10

DAILY PLANNER

Today's goals

Mood:

😆 😊 😐 😟 😢

Water Intake:

💧 💧 💧 💧 💧 💧 💧

Priorities with Consequences

A⁺

A⁺

A⁺

Things to get done today:

_____
_____
_____
_____
_____
_____
_____
_____

Today's appointment:

TIME:	EVENT:

For tomorrow:

_____
_____
_____
_____

		1	2	3	4	5	6	7	8	9	10
IMPULSIVITY	Easily Frustrated	1	2	3	4	5	6	7	8	9	10
	Acting Without Thikining	1	2	3	4	5	6	7	8	9	10
	Interrupting Others	1	2	3	4	5	6	7	8	9	10
	Emotional Outbursts	1	2	3	4	5	6	7	8	9	10
HYPERACTIVITY	Difficulty Sleeping	1	2	3	4	5	6	7	8	9	10
	Constantly Moving	1	2	3	4	5	6	7	8	9	10
	Unable to Sit Still / Fidgeting	1	2	3	4	5	6	7	8	9	10
	Excessive Talking	1	2	3	4	5	6	7	8	9	10
INATTENTION	Easily Distracted	1	2	3	4	5	6	7	8	9	10
	Careless Mistakes	1	2	3	4	5	6	7	8	9	10
	Short Attention	1	2	3	4	5	6	7	8	9	10
	Forgetfulness	1	2	3	4	5	6	7	8	9	10

Date _____

DAILY PLANNER

TODAY'S GOALS

MOOD:

WATER INTAKE:

PRIORITIES WITH CONSEQUENCES

A⁺

A⁺

A⁺

THINGS TO GET DONE TODAY:

TODAY'S APPOINTMENT:

TIME: EVENT:

FOR TOMORROW:

		1	2	3	4	5	6	7	8	9	10
IMPULSIVITY	Easily Frustrated	1	2	3	4	5	6	7	8	9	10
	Acting Without Thikining	1	2	3	4	5	6	7	8	9	10
	Interrupting Others	1	2	3	4	5	6	7	8	9	10
	Emotional Outbursts	1	2	3	4	5	6	7	8	9	10
HYPERACTIVITY	Difficulty Sleeping	1	2	3	4	5	6	7	8	9	10
	Constantly Moving	1	2	3	4	5	6	7	8	9	10
	Unable to Sit Still / Fidgeting	1	2	3	4	5	6	7	8	9	10
	Excessive Talking	1	2	3	4	5	6	7	8	9	10
INATTENTION	Easily Distracted	1	2	3	4	5	6	7	8	9	10
	Careless Mistakes	1	2	3	4	5	6	7	8	9	10
	Short Attention	1	2	3	4	5	6	7	8	9	10
	Forgetfulness	1	2	3	4	5	6	7	8	9	10

Date _____

DAILY PLANNER

Today's goals

Mood:

😄 🙂 😐 🙁 😢

Water Intake:

💧 💧 💧 💧 💧 💧 💧 💧

Priorities with Consequences

A⁺

A⁺

A⁺

Things to get done today:

_____
_____
_____
_____
_____
_____
_____
_____
_____

Today's appointment:

TIME:	EVENT:

For tomorrow:

_____
_____
_____
_____
_____

		1	2	3	4	5	6	7	8	9	10
IMPULSIVITY	Easily Frustrated	1	2	3	4	5	6	7	8	9	10
	Acting Without Thikining	1	2	3	4	5	6	7	8	9	10
	Interrupting Others	1	2	3	4	5	6	7	8	9	10
	Emotional Outbursts	1	2	3	4	5	6	7	8	9	10
HYPERACTIVITY	Difficulty Sleeping	1	2	3	4	5	6	7	8	9	10
	Constantly Moving	1	2	3	4	5	6	7	8	9	10
	Unable to Sit Still / Fidgeting	1	2	3	4	5	6	7	8	9	10
	Excessive Talking	1	2	3	4	5	6	7	8	9	10
INATTENTION	Easily Distracted	1	2	3	4	5	6	7	8	9	10
	Careless Mistakes	1	2	3	4	5	6	7	8	9	10
	Short Attention	1	2	3	4	5	6	7	8	9	10
	Forgetfulness	1	2	3	4	5	6	7	8	9	10

DAILY PLANNER

TODAY'S GOALS

MOOD:

PRIORITIES WITH CONSEQUENCES

A+

WATER INTAKE:

A+

THINGS TO GET DONE TODAY:

_____

_____

_____

_____

_____

_____

_____

_____

TODAY'S APPOINTMENT:

TIME:	EVENT:

A+

FOR TOMORROW:

_____

_____

_____

_____

		1	2	3	4	5	6	7	8	9	10
IMPULSIVITY	Easily Frustrated	1	2	3	4	5	6	7	8	9	10
	Acting Without Thikining	1	2	3	4	5	6	7	8	9	10
	Interrupting Others	1	2	3	4	5	6	7	8	9	10
	Emotional Outbursts	1	2	3	4	5	6	7	8	9	10
HYPERACTIVITY	Difficulty Sleeping	1	2	3	4	5	6	7	8	9	10
	Constantly Moving	1	2	3	4	5	6	7	8	9	10
	Unable to Sit Still / Fidgeting	1	2	3	4	5	6	7	8	9	10
	Excessive Talking	1	2	3	4	5	6	7	8	9	10
INATTENTION	Easily Distracted	1	2	3	4	5	6	7	8	9	10
	Careless Mistakes	1	2	3	4	5	6	7	8	9	10
	Short Attention	1	2	3	4	5	6	7	8	9	10
	Forgetfulness	1	2	3	4	5	6	7	8	9	10

Date _____

DAILY PLANNER

TODAY'S GOALS

MOOD:

😄 🙂 😐 🙁 😢

WATER INTAKE:

◇ ◇ ◇ ◇ ◇ ◇ ◇ ◇

PRIORITIES WITH CONSEQUENCES

A⁺

A⁺

A⁺

THINGS TO GET DONE TODAY:

_____
_____
_____
_____
_____
_____
_____
_____

TODAY'S APPOINTMENT:

TIME:	EVENT:

FOR TOMORROW:

_____
_____
_____
_____
_____

IMPULSIVITY	Easily Frustrated	1	2	3	4	5	6	7	8	9	10
	Acting Without Thikining	1	2	3	4	5	6	7	8	9	10
	Interrupting Others	1	2	3	4	5	6	7	8	9	10
	Emotional Outbursts	1	2	3	4	5	6	7	8	9	10
HYPERACTIVITY	Difficulty Sleeping	1	2	3	4	5	6	7	8	9	10
	Constantly Moving	1	2	3	4	5	6	7	8	9	10
	Unable to Sit Still / Fidgeting	1	2	3	4	5	6	7	8	9	10
	Excessive Talking	1	2	3	4	5	6	7	8	9	10
INATTENTION	Easily Distracted	1	2	3	4	5	6	7	8	9	10
	Careless Mistakes	1	2	3	4	5	6	7	8	9	10
	Short Attention	1	2	3	4	5	6	7	8	9	10
	Forgetfulness	1	2	3	4	5	6	7	8	9	10

MEDICATION
Tracker

	MEDICATION	DOSAGE	FREQUENCY	TAKEN
MONDAY				
TUESDAY				
WEDNESDAY				
THURSDAY				
FRIDAY				
SATURDAY				
SUNDAY				

NOTES

Nothing like ADHD and a good
fight to the death to make time fly.

—RICK RIORDAN

TO DO'S

Weekly

MUST DO!

_____

_____

_____

IMPORTANT

_____

_____

_____

_____

_____

_____

_____

_____

_____

_____

LESS IMPORTANT

_____

_____

_____

_____

_____

_____

_____

_____

_____

_____

NOTES

_____   _____

_____   _____

_____   _____

_____   _____

In the power of fixing the attention lies the
most precious of the intellectual habits.
– ROBERT HALL

HABIT TRACKER
Weekly

HÁBITS	MON	TUES	WED	THU	FRI	SAT	SUN
	○	○	○	○	○	○	○
	○	○	○	○	○	○	○
	○	○	○	○	○	○	○
	○	○	○	○	○	○	○
	○	○	○	○	○	○	○
	○	○	○	○	○	○	○
	○	○	○	○	○	○	○
	○	○	○	○	○	○	○
	○	○	○	○	○	○	○
	○	○	○	○	○	○	○
	○	○	○	○	○	○	○
	○	○	○	○	○	○	○
	○	○	○	○	○	○	○

HOW DID I DO?

"I have more thoughts before breakfast
than most people have all day."
— UNKNOWN

BRAIN DUMP

Though Organizer

MUST DO	SHOULD DO
COULD START	**MUST DO**

Date _____

DAILY PLANNER

Today's goals

Mood:

Priorities with Consequences

Water Intake:

A⁺

A⁺

Things to get done today:

Today's appointment:

A⁺

_____
_____
_____
_____
_____
_____
_____
_____
_____
_____
_____

TIME:	EVENT:

For tomorrow:

_____
_____
_____
_____
_____

		1	2	3	4	5	6	7	8	9	10
IMPULSIVITY	Easily Frustrated	1	2	3	4	5	6	7	8	9	10
	Acting Without Thikining	1	2	3	4	5	6	7	8	9	10
	Interrupting Others	1	2	3	4	5	6	7	8	9	10
	Emotional Outbursts	1	2	3	4	5	6	7	8	9	10
HYPERACTIVITY	Difficulty Sleeping	1	2	3	4	5	6	7	8	9	10
	Constantly Moving	1	2	3	4	5	6	7	8	9	10
	Unable to Sit Still / Fidgeting	1	2	3	4	5	6	7	8	9	10
	Excessive Talking	1	2	3	4	5	6	7	8	9	10
INATTENTION	Easily Distracted	1	2	3	4	5	6	7	8	9	10
	Careless Mistakes	1	2	3	4	5	6	7	8	9	10
	Short Attention	1	2	3	4	5	6	7	8	9	10
	Forgetfulness	1	2	3	4	5	6	7	8	9	10

Date _____

DAILY PLANNER

Today's Goals

Mood:

😄 🙂 😐 🙁 😢

Water Intake:

Priorities with Consequences

A⁺

A⁺

A⁺

Things to get done today:

_____
_____
_____
_____
_____
_____
_____
_____

Today's appointment:

TIME:	EVENT:

For tomorrow:

_____
_____
_____
_____
_____

		1	2	3	4	5	6	7	8	9	10
IMPULSIVITY	Easily Frustrated	1	2	3	4	5	6	7	8	9	10
	Acting Without Thikining	1	2	3	4	5	6	7	8	9	10
	Interrupting Others	1	2	3	4	5	6	7	8	9	10
	Emotional Outbursts	1	2	3	4	5	6	7	8	9	10
HYPERACTIVITY	Difficulty Sleeping	1	2	3	4	5	6	7	8	9	10
	Constantly Moving	1	2	3	4	5	6	7	8	9	10
	Unable to Sit Still / Fidgeting	1	2	3	4	5	6	7	8	9	10
	Excessive Talking	1	2	3	4	5	6	7	8	9	10
INATTENTION	Easily Distracted	1	2	3	4	5	6	7	8	9	10
	Careless Mistakes	1	2	3	4	5	6	7	8	9	10
	Short Attention	1	2	3	4	5	6	7	8	9	10
	Forgetfulness	1	2	3	4	5	6	7	8	9	10

Date _____

DAILY PLANNER

Today's goals

Mood:

Priorities with Consequences

A⁺

Water Intake:

A⁺

Things to get done today:

_____
_____
_____
_____
_____
_____
_____
_____

Today's appointment:

TIME:	EVENT:

A⁺

For tomorrow:

_____
_____
_____
_____
_____
_____

		1	2	3	4	5	6	7	8	9	10
IMPULSIVITY	Easily Frustrated	1	2	3	4	5	6	7	8	9	10
	Acting Without Thikining	1	2	3	4	5	6	7	8	9	10
	Interrupting Others	1	2	3	4	5	6	7	8	9	10
	Emotional Outbursts	1	2	3	4	5	6	7	8	9	10
HYPERACTIVITY	Difficulty Sleeping	1	2	3	4	5	6	7	8	9	10
	Constantly Moving	1	2	3	4	5	6	7	8	9	10
	Unable to Sit Still / Fidgeting	1	2	3	4	5	6	7	8	9	10
	Excessive Talking	1	2	3	4	5	6	7	8	9	10
INATTENTION	Easily Distracted	1	2	3	4	5	6	7	8	9	10
	Careless Mistakes	1	2	3	4	5	6	7	8	9	10
	Short Attention	1	2	3	4	5	6	7	8	9	10
	Forgetfulness	1	2	3	4	5	6	7	8	9	10

Date _____

DAILY PLANNER

Today's Goals

Mood:

Water Intake:

Priorities with Consequences

A⁺

A⁺

A⁺

Things to get done today:

Today's appointment:

TIME: EVENT:

For tomorrow:

		1	2	3	4	5	6	7	8	9	10
IMPULSIVITY	Easily Frustrated	1	2	3	4	5	6	7	8	9	10
	Acting Without Thikining	1	2	3	4	5	6	7	8	9	10
	Interrupting Others	1	2	3	4	5	6	7	8	9	10
	Emotional Outbursts	1	2	3	4	5	6	7	8	9	10
HYPERACTIVITY	Difficulty Sleeping	1	2	3	4	5	6	7	8	9	10
	Constantly Moving	1	2	3	4	5	6	7	8	9	10
	Unable to Sit Still / Fidgeting	1	2	3	4	5	6	7	8	9	10
	Excessive Talking	1	2	3	4	5	6	7	8	9	10
INATTENTION	Easily Distracted	1	2	3	4	5	6	7	8	9	10
	Careless Mistakes	1	2	3	4	5	6	7	8	9	10
	Short Attention	1	2	3	4	5	6	7	8	9	10
	Forgetfulness	1	2	3	4	5	6	7	8	9	10

DAILY PLANNER

TODAY'S GOALS

MOOD:

WATER INTAKE:

PRIORITIES WITH CONSEQUENCES

A⁺

A⁺

THINGS TO GET DONE TODAY:

_____
_____
_____
_____
_____
_____
_____
_____
_____
_____
_____

TODAY'S APPOINTMENT:

TIME: EVENT:

A⁺

FOR TOMORROW:

_____
_____
_____
_____
_____
_____

		1	2	3	4	5	6	7	8	9	10
IMPULSIVITY	Easily Frustrated	1	2	3	4	5	6	7	8	9	10
	Acting Without Thikining	1	2	3	4	5	6	7	8	9	10
	Interrupting Others	1	2	3	4	5	6	7	8	9	10
	Emotional Outbursts	1	2	3	4	5	6	7	8	9	10
HYPERACTIVITY	Difficulty Sleeping	1	2	3	4	5	6	7	8	9	10
	Constantly Moving	1	2	3	4	5	6	7	8	9	10
	Unable to Sit Still / Fidgeting	1	2	3	4	5	6	7	8	9	10
	Excessive Talking	1	2	3	4	5	6	7	8	9	10
INATTENTION	Easily Distracted	1	2	3	4	5	6	7	8	9	10
	Careless Mistakes	1	2	3	4	5	6	7	8	9	10
	Short Attention	1	2	3	4	5	6	7	8	9	10
	Forgetfulness	1	2	3	4	5	6	7	8	9	10

Date _____

DAILY PLANNER

Today's goals

Mood:

🙂 🙂 😐 🙁 😢

Water Intake:

⬡ ⬡ ⬡ ⬡ ⬡ ⬡ ⬡

Priorities with Consequences

A⁺

A⁺

A⁺

Things to get done today:

_____
_____
_____
_____
_____
_____
_____
_____
_____

Today's appointment:

TIME:	EVENT:

For tomorrow:

_____
_____
_____
_____
_____

		1	2	3	4	5	6	7	8	9	10
IMPULSIVITY	Easily Frustrated	1	2	3	4	5	6	7	8	9	10
	Acting Without Thikining	1	2	3	4	5	6	7	8	9	10
	Interrupting Others	1	2	3	4	5	6	7	8	9	10
	Emotional Outbursts	1	2	3	4	5	6	7	8	9	10
HYPERACTIVITY	Difficulty Sleeping	1	2	3	4	5	6	7	8	9	10
	Constantly Moving	1	2	3	4	5	6	7	8	9	10
	Unable to Sit Still / Fidgeting	1	2	3	4	5	6	7	8	9	10
	Excessive Talking	1	2	3	4	5	6	7	8	9	10
INATTENTION	Easily Distracted	1	2	3	4	5	6	7	8	9	10
	Careless Mistakes	1	2	3	4	5	6	7	8	9	10
	Short Attention	1	2	3	4	5	6	7	8	9	10
	Forgetfulness	1	2	3	4	5	6	7	8	9	10

DAILY PLANNER

Today's goals

Mood:

Priorities with Consequences

Water Intake:

Things to get done today:

_____
_____
_____
_____
_____
_____
_____
_____
_____

Today's appointment:

TIME: EVENT:

For tomorrow:

_____
_____
_____
_____
_____

		1	2	3	4	5	6	7	8	9	10
IMPULSIVITY	Easily Frustrated	1	2	3	4	5	6	7	8	9	10
	Acting Without Thikining	1	2	3	4	5	6	7	8	9	10
	Interrupting Others	1	2	3	4	5	6	7	8	9	10
	Emotional Outbursts	1	2	3	4	5	6	7	8	9	10
HYPERACTIVITY	Difficulty Sleeping	1	2	3	4	5	6	7	8	9	10
	Constantly Moving	1	2	3	4	5	6	7	8	9	10
	Unable to Sit Still / Fidgeting	1	2	3	4	5	6	7	8	9	10
	Excessive Talking	1	2	3	4	5	6	7	8	9	10
INATTENTION	Easily Distracted	1	2	3	4	5	6	7	8	9	10
	Careless Mistakes	1	2	3	4	5	6	7	8	9	10
	Short Attention	1	2	3	4	5	6	7	8	9	10
	Forgetfulness	1	2	3	4	5	6	7	8	9	10

MEDICATION
Tracker

	MEDICATION	DOSAGE	FREQUENCY	TAKEN
MONDAY				
TUESDAY				
WEDNESDAY				
THURSDAY				
FRIDAY				
SATURDAY				
SUNDAY				

NOTES

TO DO'S
Weekly

MUST DO!

_____
_____
_____

IMPORTANT

- _____
- _____
- _____
- _____
- _____
- _____
- _____
- _____
- _____
- _____
- _____

LESS IMPORTANT

- _____
- _____
- _____
- _____
- _____
- _____
- _____
- _____
- _____
- _____
- _____

NOTES

_____   _____
_____   _____
_____   _____
_____   _____

In the power of fixing the attention lies the
most precious of the intellectual habits.
– ROBERT HALL

HABIT TRACKER
Weekly

HÁBITS	MON	TUES	WED	THU	FRI	SAT	SUN
_____	○	○	○	○	○	○	○
_____	○	○	○	○	○	○	○
_____	○	○	○	○	○	○	○
_____	○	○	○	○	○	○	○
_____	○	○	○	○	○	○	○
_____	○	○	○	○	○	○	○
_____	○	○	○	○	○	○	○
_____	○	○	○	○	○	○	○
_____	○	○	○	○	○	○	○
_____	○	○	○	○	○	○	○
_____	○	○	○	○	○	○	○
_____	○	○	○	○	○	○	○
_____	○	○	○	○	○	○	○
_____	○	○	○	○	○	○	○
_____	○	○	○	○	○	○	○

HOW DID I DO?

"I have more thoughts before breakfast
than most people have all day."
— UNKNOWN

BRAIN DUMP

Though Organizer

MUST DO	SHOULD DO
COULD START	MUST DO

Date _____

DAILY PLANNER

Today's goals

Mood:
😄 🙂 😐 🙁 😞

Water Intake:
💧💧💧💧💧💧💧

Priorities with Consequences
A⁺

A⁺

A⁺

Things to get done today:
_____
_____
_____
_____
_____
_____
_____
_____
_____

Today's appointment:
TIME: EVENT:

For tomorrow:
_____
_____
_____
_____
_____

		1	2	3	4	5	6	7	8	9	10
IMPULSIVITY	Easily Frustrated	1	2	3	4	5	6	7	8	9	10
	Acting Without Thikining	1	2	3	4	5	6	7	8	9	10
	Interrupting Others	1	2	3	4	5	6	7	8	9	10
	Emotional Outbursts	1	2	3	4	5	6	7	8	9	10
HYPERACTIVITY	Difficulty Sleeping	1	2	3	4	5	6	7	8	9	10
	Constantly Moving	1	2	3	4	5	6	7	8	9	10
	Unable to Sit Still / Fidgeting	1	2	3	4	5	6	7	8	9	10
	Excessive Talking	1	2	3	4	5	6	7	8	9	10
INATTENTION	Easily Distracted	1	2	3	4	5	6	7	8	9	10
	Careless Mistakes	1	2	3	4	5	6	7	8	9	10
	Short Attention	1	2	3	4	5	6	7	8	9	10
	Forgetfulness	1	2	3	4	5	6	7	8	9	10

Date _____

DAILY PLANNER

Today's goals

Mood:

Water Intake:

Priorities with Consequences

A⁺

A⁺

A⁺

Things to get done today:

Today's appointment:

TIME: EVENT:

For tomorrow:

		1	2	3	4	5	6	7	8	9	10
IMPULSIVITY	Easily Frustrated	1	2	3	4	5	6	7	8	9	10
	Acting Without Thikining	1	2	3	4	5	6	7	8	9	10
	Interrupting Others	1	2	3	4	5	6	7	8	9	10
	Emotional Outbursts	1	2	3	4	5	6	7	8	9	10
HYPERACTIVITY	Difficulty Sleeping	1	2	3	4	5	6	7	8	9	10
	Constantly Moving	1	2	3	4	5	6	7	8	9	10
	Unable to Sit Still / Fidgeting	1	2	3	4	5	6	7	8	9	10
	Excessive Talking	1	2	3	4	5	6	7	8	9	10
INATTENTION	Easily Distracted	1	2	3	4	5	6	7	8	9	10
	Careless Mistakes	1	2	3	4	5	6	7	8	9	10
	Short Attention	1	2	3	4	5	6	7	8	9	10
	Forgetfulness	1	2	3	4	5	6	7	8	9	10

 *Date* _____

DAILY PLANNER

Today's goals

Mood:

Priorities with Consequences

A⁺

Water Intake:

A⁺

Things to get done today:

Today's appointment:

A⁺

TIME: EVENT:

For tomorrow:

		1	2	3	4	5	6	7	8	9	10
IMPULSIVITY	Easily Frustrated	1	2	3	4	5	6	7	8	9	10
	Acting Without Thikining	1	2	3	4	5	6	7	8	9	10
	Interrupting Others	1	2	3	4	5	6	7	8	9	10
	Emotional Outbursts	1	2	3	4	5	6	7	8	9	10
HYPERACTIVITY	Difficulty Sleeping	1	2	3	4	5	6	7	8	9	10
	Constantly Moving	1	2	3	4	5	6	7	8	9	10
	Unable to Sit Still / Fidgeting	1	2	3	4	5	6	7	8	9	10
	Excessive Talking	1	2	3	4	5	6	7	8	9	10
INATTENTION	Easily Distracted	1	2	3	4	5	6	7	8	9	10
	Careless Mistakes	1	2	3	4	5	6	7	8	9	10
	Short Attention	1	2	3	4	5	6	7	8	9	10
	Forgetfulness	1	2	3	4	5	6	7	8	9	10

Date _____

DAILY PLANNER

TODAY'S GOALS

MOOD:

WATER INTAKE:

PRIORITIES WITH CONSEQUENCES

A⁺

A⁺

A⁺

THINGS TO GET DONE TODAY:

_____
_____
_____
_____
_____
_____
_____
_____
_____

TODAY'S APPOINTMENT:

TIME: EVENT:

FOR TOMORROW:

_____
_____
_____
_____
_____

		1	2	3	4	5	6	7	8	9	10
IMPULSIVITY	Easily Frustrated	1	2	3	4	5	6	7	8	9	10
	Acting Without Thikining	1	2	3	4	5	6	7	8	9	10
	Interrupting Others	1	2	3	4	5	6	7	8	9	10
	Emotional Outbursts	1	2	3	4	5	6	7	8	9	10
HYPERACTIVITY	Difficulty Sleeping	1	2	3	4	5	6	7	8	9	10
	Constantly Moving	1	2	3	4	5	6	7	8	9	10
	Unable to Sit Still / Fidgeting	1	2	3	4	5	6	7	8	9	10
	Excessive Talking	1	2	3	4	5	6	7	8	9	10
INATTENTION	Easily Distracted	1	2	3	4	5	6	7	8	9	10
	Careless Mistakes	1	2	3	4	5	6	7	8	9	10
	Short Attention	1	2	3	4	5	6	7	8	9	10
	Forgetfulness	1	2	3	4	5	6	7	8	9	10

Date _____

DAILY PLANNER

TODAY'S GOALS

MOOD:

PRIORITIES WITH CONSEQUENCES

A⁺

WATER INTAKE:

A⁺

THINGS TO GET DONE TODAY:

TODAY'S APPOINTMENT:

A⁺

TIME: EVENT:

FOR TOMORROW:

		1	2	3	4	5	6	7	8	9	10
IMPULSIVITY	Easily Frustrated	1	2	3	4	5	6	7	8	9	10
	Acting Without Thikining	1	2	3	4	5	6	7	8	9	10
	Interrupting Others	1	2	3	4	5	6	7	8	9	10
	Emotional Outbursts	1	2	3	4	5	6	7	8	9	10
HYPERACTIVITY	Difficulty Sleeping	1	2	3	4	5	6	7	8	9	10
	Constantly Moving	1	2	3	4	5	6	7	8	9	10
	Unable to Sit Still / Fidgeting	1	2	3	4	5	6	7	8	9	10
	Excessive Talking	1	2	3	4	5	6	7	8	9	10
INATTENTION	Easily Distracted	1	2	3	4	5	6	7	8	9	10
	Careless Mistakes	1	2	3	4	5	6	7	8	9	10
	Short Attention	1	2	3	4	5	6	7	8	9	10
	Forgetfulness	1	2	3	4	5	6	7	8	9	10

 *Date* _____

DAILY PLANNER

⊙ Today's goals

Mood:
😊 🙂 😐 🙁 😢

Water Intake:
💧 💧 💧 💧 💧 💧 💧

Priorities with Consequences
A⁺

A⁺

A⁺

Things to get done today:
_____
_____
_____
_____
_____
_____
_____
_____

Today's appointment:
TIME:	EVENT:

For tomorrow:
_____
_____
_____
_____
_____

		1	2	3	4	5	6	7	8	9	10
IMPULSIVITY	Easily Frustrated	1	2	3	4	5	6	7	8	9	10
	Acting Without Thikining	1	2	3	4	5	6	7	8	9	10
	Interrupting Others	1	2	3	4	5	6	7	8	9	10
	Emotional Outbursts	1	2	3	4	5	6	7	8	9	10
HYPERACTIVITY	Difficulty Sleeping	1	2	3	4	5	6	7	8	9	10
	Constantly Moving	1	2	3	4	5	6	7	8	9	10
	Unable to Sit Still / Fidgeting	1	2	3	4	5	6	7	8	9	10
	Excessive Talking	1	2	3	4	5	6	7	8	9	10
INATTENTION	Easily Distracted	1	2	3	4	5	6	7	8	9	10
	Careless Mistakes	1	2	3	4	5	6	7	8	9	10
	Short Attention	1	2	3	4	5	6	7	8	9	10
	Forgetfulness	1	2	3	4	5	6	7	8	9	10

Date _____

DAILY PLANNER

TODAY'S GOALS

MOOD:

WATER INTAKE:

PRIORITIES WITH CONSEQUENCES

A⁺

A⁺

A⁺

THINGS TO GET DONE TODAY:

_____
_____
_____
_____
_____
_____
_____
_____
_____

TODAY'S APPOINTMENT:

TIME:	EVENT:

FOR TOMORROW:

_____
_____
_____
_____
_____

		1	2	3	4	5	6	7	8	9	10
IMPULSIVITY	Easily Frustrated	1	2	3	4	5	6	7	8	9	10
	Acting Without Thikining	1	2	3	4	5	6	7	8	9	10
	Interrupting Others	1	2	3	4	5	6	7	8	9	10
	Emotional Outbursts	1	2	3	4	5	6	7	8	9	10
HYPERACTIVITY	Difficulty Sleeping	1	2	3	4	5	6	7	8	9	10
	Constantly Moving	1	2	3	4	5	6	7	8	9	10
	Unable to Sit Still / Fidgeting	1	2	3	4	5	6	7	8	9	10
	Excessive Talking	1	2	3	4	5	6	7	8	9	10
INATTENTION	Easily Distracted	1	2	3	4	5	6	7	8	9	10
	Careless Mistakes	1	2	3	4	5	6	7	8	9	10
	Short Attention	1	2	3	4	5	6	7	8	9	10
	Forgetfulness	1	2	3	4	5	6	7	8	9	10

MEDICATION
Tracker

	MEDICATION	DOSAGE	FREQUENCY	TAKEN
MONDAY				
TUESDAY				
WEDNESDAY				
THURSDAY				
FRIDAY				
SATURDAY				
SUNDAY				

NOTES

TO DO'S
Weekly

Must Do!

_____

_____

_____

Important

- _____
- _____
- _____
- _____
- _____
- _____
- _____
- _____
- _____
- _____

Less important

- _____
- _____
- _____
- _____
- _____
- _____
- _____
- _____
- _____
- _____

Notes

_____ _____

_____ _____

_____ _____

_____ _____

In the power of fixing the attention lies the
most precious of the intellectual habits.
– Robert Hall

HABIT TRACKER
Weekly

HÁBITS	MON	TUES	WED	THU	FRI	SAT	SUN
_____	◯	◯	◯	◯	◯	◯	◯
_____	◯	◯	◯	◯	◯	◯	◯
_____	◯	◯	◯	◯	◯	◯	◯
_____	◯	◯	◯	◯	◯	◯	◯
_____	◯	◯	◯	◯	◯	◯	◯
_____	◯	◯	◯	◯	◯	◯	◯
_____	◯	◯	◯	◯	◯	◯	◯
_____	◯	◯	◯	◯	◯	◯	◯
_____	◯	◯	◯	◯	◯	◯	◯
_____	◯	◯	◯	◯	◯	◯	◯
_____	◯	◯	◯	◯	◯	◯	◯
_____	◯	◯	◯	◯	◯	◯	◯
_____	◯	◯	◯	◯	◯	◯	◯
_____	◯	◯	◯	◯	◯	◯	◯

HOW DID I DO?

"I have more thoughts before breakfast
than most people have all day."
— UNKNOWN

BRAIN DUMP
Though Organizer

MUST DO	SHOULD DO

COULD START	MUST DO

DAILY PLANNER

Today's goals

Mood:

Water Intake:

Priorities with Consequences

A⁺

A⁺

A⁺

Things to get done today:

_____
_____
_____
_____
_____
_____
_____
_____
_____
_____

Today's appointment:

TIME:	EVENT:

For tomorrow:

_____
_____
_____
_____
_____

		1	2	3	4	5	6	7	8	9	10
IMPULSIVITY	Easily Frustrated	1	2	3	4	5	6	7	8	9	10
	Acting Without Thikining	1	2	3	4	5	6	7	8	9	10
	Interrupting Others	1	2	3	4	5	6	7	8	9	10
	Emotional Outbursts	1	2	3	4	5	6	7	8	9	10
HYPERACTIVITY	Difficulty Sleeping	1	2	3	4	5	6	7	8	9	10
	Constantly Moving	1	2	3	4	5	6	7	8	9	10
	Unable to Sit Still / Fidgeting	1	2	3	4	5	6	7	8	9	10
	Excessive Talking	1	2	3	4	5	6	7	8	9	10
INATTENTION	Easily Distracted	1	2	3	4	5	6	7	8	9	10
	Careless Mistakes	1	2	3	4	5	6	7	8	9	10
	Short Attention	1	2	3	4	5	6	7	8	9	10
	Forgetfulness	1	2	3	4	5	6	7	8	9	10

Date _____

DAILY PLANNER

Today's goals

Mood:

Water Intake:

Priorities with Consequences

Things to get done today:

_____
_____
_____
_____
_____
_____
_____
_____

Today's appointment:

TIME: EVENT:

For tomorrow:

_____
_____
_____
_____

		1	2	3	4	5	6	7	8	9	10
IMPULSIVITY	Easily Frustrated	1	2	3	4	5	6	7	8	9	10
	Acting Without Thikining	1	2	3	4	5	6	7	8	9	10
	Interrupting Others	1	2	3	4	5	6	7	8	9	10
	Emotional Outbursts	1	2	3	4	5	6	7	8	9	10
HYPERACTIVITY	Difficulty Sleeping	1	2	3	4	5	6	7	8	9	10
	Constantly Moving	1	2	3	4	5	6	7	8	9	10
	Unable to Sit Still / Fidgeting	1	2	3	4	5	6	7	8	9	10
	Excessive Talking	1	2	3	4	5	6	7	8	9	10
INATTENTION	Easily Distracted	1	2	3	4	5	6	7	8	9	10
	Careless Mistakes	1	2	3	4	5	6	7	8	9	10
	Short Attention	1	2	3	4	5	6	7	8	9	10
	Forgetfulness	1	2	3	4	5	6	7	8	9	10

Date _____

DAILY PLANNER

Today's Goals

Mood:

😄 🙂 😐 🙁 😢

Water Intake:

💧💧💧💧💧💧💧

Priorities with Consequences

A+

A+

A+

Things to get done today:

_____
_____
_____
_____
_____
_____
_____
_____
_____

Today's appointment:

TIME:	EVENT:

For tomorrow:

_____
_____
_____
_____
_____

		1	2	3	4	5	6	7	8	9	10
IMPULSIVITY	Easily Frustrated	1	2	3	4	5	6	7	8	9	10
	Acting Without Thikining	1	2	3	4	5	6	7	8	9	10
	Interrupting Others	1	2	3	4	5	6	7	8	9	10
	Emotional Outbursts	1	2	3	4	5	6	7	8	9	10
HYPERACTIVITY	Difficulty Sleeping	1	2	3	4	5	6	7	8	9	10
	Constantly Moving	1	2	3	4	5	6	7	8	9	10
	Unable to Sit Still / Fidgeting	1	2	3	4	5	6	7	8	9	10
	Excessive Talking	1	2	3	4	5	6	7	8	9	10
INATTENTION	Easily Distracted	1	2	3	4	5	6	7	8	9	10
	Careless Mistakes	1	2	3	4	5	6	7	8	9	10
	Short Attention	1	2	3	4	5	6	7	8	9	10
	Forgetfulness	1	2	3	4	5	6	7	8	9	10

 Date _____

DAILY PLANNER

Today's goals

Mood:

Water Intake:

Priorities with Consequences

Things to get done today:

_____
_____
_____
_____
_____
_____
_____
_____
_____

Today's appointment:

TIME:	EVENT:

For tomorrow:

_____
_____
_____
_____
_____

		1	2	3	4	5	6	7	8	9	10
IMPULSIVITY	Easily Frustrated	1	2	3	4	5	6	7	8	9	10
	Acting Without Thikining	1	2	3	4	5	6	7	8	9	10
	Interrupting Others	1	2	3	4	5	6	7	8	9	10
	Emotional Outbursts	1	2	3	4	5	6	7	8	9	10
HYPERACTIVITY	Difficulty Sleeping	1	2	3	4	5	6	7	8	9	10
	Constantly Moving	1	2	3	4	5	6	7	8	9	10
	Unable to Sit Still / Fidgeting	1	2	3	4	5	6	7	8	9	10
	Excessive Talking	1	2	3	4	5	6	7	8	9	10
INATTENTION	Easily Distracted	1	2	3	4	5	6	7	8	9	10
	Careless Mistakes	1	2	3	4	5	6	7	8	9	10
	Short Attention	1	2	3	4	5	6	7	8	9	10
	Forgetfulness	1	2	3	4	5	6	7	8	9	10

DAILY PLANNER

Today's goals

Mood:

Priorities with Consequences

Water Intake:

Things to get done today:

Today's appointment:

TIME:	EVENT:

For tomorrow:

		1	2	3	4	5	6	7	8	9	10
IMPULSIVITY	Easily Frustrated	1	2	3	4	5	6	7	8	9	10
	Acting Without Thikining	1	2	3	4	5	6	7	8	9	10
	Interrupting Others	1	2	3	4	5	6	7	8	9	10
	Emotional Outbursts	1	2	3	4	5	6	7	8	9	10
HYPERACTIVITY	Difficulty Sleeping	1	2	3	4	5	6	7	8	9	10
	Constantly Moving	1	2	3	4	5	6	7	8	9	10
	Unable to Sit Still / Fidgeting	1	2	3	4	5	6	7	8	9	10
	Excessive Talking	1	2	3	4	5	6	7	8	9	10
INATTENTION	Easily Distracted	1	2	3	4	5	6	7	8	9	10
	Careless Mistakes	1	2	3	4	5	6	7	8	9	10
	Short Attention	1	2	3	4	5	6	7	8	9	10
	Forgetfulness	1	2	3	4	5	6	7	8	9	10

DAILY PLANNER

Today's goals

Mood:

😃 🙂 😐 🙁 😢

Water Intake:

◇ ◇ ◇ ◇ ◇ ◇ ◇

Priorities with Consequences

A⁺

A⁺

A⁺

Things to get done today:

Today's appointment:

TIME: EVENT:

For tomorrow:

		1	2	3	4	5	6	7	8	9	10
IMPULSIVITY	Easily Frustrated	1	2	3	4	5	6	7	8	9	10
	Acting Without Thikining	1	2	3	4	5	6	7	8	9	10
	Interrupting Others	1	2	3	4	5	6	7	8	9	10
	Emotional Outbursts	1	2	3	4	5	6	7	8	9	10
HYPERACTIVITY	Difficulty Sleeping	1	2	3	4	5	6	7	8	9	10
	Constantly Moving	1	2	3	4	5	6	7	8	9	10
	Unable to Sit Still / Fidgeting	1	2	3	4	5	6	7	8	9	10
	Excessive Talking	1	2	3	4	5	6	7	8	9	10
INATTENTION	Easily Distracted	1	2	3	4	5	6	7	8	9	10
	Careless Mistakes	1	2	3	4	5	6	7	8	9	10
	Short Attention	1	2	3	4	5	6	7	8	9	10
	Forgetfulness	1	2	3	4	5	6	7	8	9	10

Date ___

DAILY PLANNER

TODAY'S GOALS

MOOD:

WATER INTAKE:

PRIORITIES WITH CONSEQUENCES

A⁺

A⁺

A⁺

THINGS TO GET DONE TODAY:

_____
_____
_____
_____
_____
_____
_____
_____
_____
_____

TODAY'S APPOINTMENT:

TIME:	EVENT:

FOR TOMORROW:

_____
_____
_____
_____
_____

		1	2	3	4	5	6	7	8	9	10
IMPULSIVITY	Easily Frustrated	1	2	3	4	5	6	7	8	9	10
	Acting Without Thikining	1	2	3	4	5	6	7	8	9	10
	Interrupting Others	1	2	3	4	5	6	7	8	9	10
	Emotional Outbursts	1	2	3	4	5	6	7	8	9	10
HYPERACTIVITY	Difficulty Sleeping	1	2	3	4	5	6	7	8	9	10
	Constantly Moving	1	2	3	4	5	6	7	8	9	10
	Unable to Sit Still / Fidgeting	1	2	3	4	5	6	7	8	9	10
	Excessive Talking	1	2	3	4	5	6	7	8	9	10
INATTENTION	Easily Distracted	1	2	3	4	5	6	7	8	9	10
	Careless Mistakes	1	2	3	4	5	6	7	8	9	10
	Short Attention	1	2	3	4	5	6	7	8	9	10
	Forgetfulness	1	2	3	4	5	6	7	8	9	10

MEDICATION
Tracker

	MEDICATION	DOSAGE	FREQUENCY	TAKEN
MONDAY				
TUESDAY				
WEDNESDAY				
THURSDAY				
FRIDAY				
SATURDAY				
SUNDAY				

NOTES

Nothing like ADHD and a good
fight to the death to make time fly.

—RICK RIORDAN

TO DO'S
Weekly

MUST DO!

_____

_____

_____

IMPORTANT

- _____
- _____
- _____
- _____
- _____
- _____
- _____
- _____
- _____
- _____

LESS IMPORTANT

- _____
- _____
- _____
- _____
- _____
- _____
- _____
- _____
- _____
- _____

NOTES

_____ _____

_____ _____

_____ _____

_____ _____

In the power of fixing the attention lies the
most precious of the intellectual habits.
— ROBERT HALL

HABIT TRACKER
Weekly

HÁBITS	MON	TUES	WED	THU	FRI	SAT	SUN
	○	○	○	○	○	○	○
	○	○	○	○	○	○	○
	○	○	○	○	○	○	○
	○	○	○	○	○	○	○
	○	○	○	○	○	○	○
	○	○	○	○	○	○	○
	○	○	○	○	○	○	○
	○	○	○	○	○	○	○
	○	○	○	○	○	○	○
	○	○	○	○	○	○	○
	○	○	○	○	○	○	○
	○	○	○	○	○	○	○
	○	○	○	○	○	○	○
	○	○	○	○	○	○	○

HOW DID I DO?

BRAIN DUMP

Though Organizer

MUST DO	SHOULD DO
COULD START	MUST DO

Date _____

DAILY PLANNER

Today's goals

Mood:

Priorities with Consequences

Water Intake:

Things to get done today:

_____
_____
_____
_____
_____
_____
_____
_____
_____
_____

Today's appointment:

TIME:	EVENT:

For tomorrow:

_____
_____
_____
_____
_____
_____

		1	2	3	4	5	6	7	8	9	10
IMPULSIVITY	Easily Frustrated	1	2	3	4	5	6	7	8	9	10
	Acting Without Thikining	1	2	3	4	5	6	7	8	9	10
	Interrupting Others	1	2	3	4	5	6	7	8	9	10
	Emotional Outbursts	1	2	3	4	5	6	7	8	9	10
HYPERACTIVITY	Difficulty Sleeping	1	2	3	4	5	6	7	8	9	10
	Constantly Moving	1	2	3	4	5	6	7	8	9	10
	Unable to Sit Still / Fidgeting	1	2	3	4	5	6	7	8	9	10
	Excessive Talking	1	2	3	4	5	6	7	8	9	10
INATTENTION	Easily Distracted	1	2	3	4	5	6	7	8	9	10
	Careless Mistakes	1	2	3	4	5	6	7	8	9	10
	Short Attention	1	2	3	4	5	6	7	8	9	10
	Forgetfulness	1	2	3	4	5	6	7	8	9	10

DAILY PLANNER

Today's goals

Mood:

😄 🙂 😐 🙁 😢

Water Intake:

Priorities with Consequences

A⁺

A⁺

A⁺

Things to get done today:

_____
_____
_____
_____
_____
_____
_____
_____

Today's appointment:

TIME:	EVENT:

For tomorrow:

_____
_____
_____
_____
_____

		1	2	3	4	5	6	7	8	9	10
IMPULSIVITY	Easily Frustrated	1	2	3	4	5	6	7	8	9	10
	Acting Without Thikining	1	2	3	4	5	6	7	8	9	10
	Interrupting Others	1	2	3	4	5	6	7	8	9	10
	Emotional Outbursts	1	2	3	4	5	6	7	8	9	10
HYPERACTIVITY	Difficulty Sleeping	1	2	3	4	5	6	7	8	9	10
	Constantly Moving	1	2	3	4	5	6	7	8	9	10
	Unable to Sit Still / Fidgeting	1	2	3	4	5	6	7	8	9	10
	Excessive Talking	1	2	3	4	5	6	7	8	9	10
INATTENTION	Easily Distracted	1	2	3	4	5	6	7	8	9	10
	Careless Mistakes	1	2	3	4	5	6	7	8	9	10
	Short Attention	1	2	3	4	5	6	7	8	9	10
	Forgetfulness	1	2	3	4	5	6	7	8	9	10

DAILY PLANNER

Today's goals

Mood:

Water Intake:

Priorities with Consequences

A⁺

A⁺

A⁺

Things to get done today:

Today's appointment:

TIME:	EVENT:

For tomorrow:

		1	2	3	4	5	6	7	8	9	10
IMPULSIVITY	Easily Frustrated	1	2	3	4	5	6	7	8	9	10
	Acting Without Thikining	1	2	3	4	5	6	7	8	9	10
	Interrupting Others	1	2	3	4	5	6	7	8	9	10
	Emotional Outbursts	1	2	3	4	5	6	7	8	9	10
HYPERACTIVITY	Difficulty Sleeping	1	2	3	4	5	6	7	8	9	10
	Constantly Moving	1	2	3	4	5	6	7	8	9	10
	Unable to Sit Still / Fidgeting	1	2	3	4	5	6	7	8	9	10
	Excessive Talking	1	2	3	4	5	6	7	8	9	10
INATTENTION	Easily Distracted	1	2	3	4	5	6	7	8	9	10
	Careless Mistakes	1	2	3	4	5	6	7	8	9	10
	Short Attention	1	2	3	4	5	6	7	8	9	10
	Forgetfulness	1	2	3	4	5	6	7	8	9	10

DAILY PLANNER

Today's Goals

Mood:

😊 🙂 😐 🙁 😢

Water Intake:

💧 💧 💧 💧 💧 💧 💧 💧

Priorities with Consequences

A⁺

A⁺

A⁺

Things to get done today:

_____
_____
_____
_____
_____
_____
_____
_____

Today's Appointment:

TIME: | EVENT:

For tomorrow:

_____
_____
_____
_____
_____

		1	2	3	4	5	6	7	8	9	10
IMPULSIVITY	Easily Frustrated	1	2	3	4	5	6	7	8	9	10
	Acting Without Thikining	1	2	3	4	5	6	7	8	9	10
	Interrupting Others	1	2	3	4	5	6	7	8	9	10
	Emotional Outbursts	1	2	3	4	5	6	7	8	9	10
HYPERACTIVITY	Difficulty Sleeping	1	2	3	4	5	6	7	8	9	10
	Constantly Moving	1	2	3	4	5	6	7	8	9	10
	Unable to Sit Still / Fidgeting	1	2	3	4	5	6	7	8	9	10
	Excessive Talking	1	2	3	4	5	6	7	8	9	10
INATTENTION	Easily Distracted	1	2	3	4	5	6	7	8	9	10
	Careless Mistakes	1	2	3	4	5	6	7	8	9	10
	Short Attention	1	2	3	4	5	6	7	8	9	10
	Forgetfulness	1	2	3	4	5	6	7	8	9	10

DAILY PLANNER

Today's goals

Mood:

Water Intake:

Priorities with Consequences

A+

A+

A+

Things to get done today:

_____
_____
_____
_____
_____
_____
_____
_____
_____

Today's appointment:

TIME: EVENT:

For tomorrow:

_____
_____
_____
_____
_____

		1	2	3	4	5	6	7	8	9	10
IMPULSIVITY	Easily Frustrated	1	2	3	4	5	6	7	8	9	10
	Acting Without Thikining	1	2	3	4	5	6	7	8	9	10
	Interrupting Others	1	2	3	4	5	6	7	8	9	10
	Emotional Outbursts	1	2	3	4	5	6	7	8	9	10
HYPERACTIVITY	Difficulty Sleeping	1	2	3	4	5	6	7	8	9	10
	Constantly Moving	1	2	3	4	5	6	7	8	9	10
	Unable to Sit Still / Fidgeting	1	2	3	4	5	6	7	8	9	10
	Excessive Talking	1	2	3	4	5	6	7	8	9	10
INATTENTION	Easily Distracted	1	2	3	4	5	6	7	8	9	10
	Careless Mistakes	1	2	3	4	5	6	7	8	9	10
	Short Attention	1	2	3	4	5	6	7	8	9	10
	Forgetfulness	1	2	3	4	5	6	7	8	9	10

Date _____

DAILY PLANNER

Today's goals

Mood:

😊 😊 😐 ☹️ 😢

Water Intake:

💧💧💧💧💧💧💧

Priorities with Consequences

A⁺

A⁺

A⁺

Things to get done today:

_____
_____
_____
_____
_____
_____
_____
_____
_____

Today's appointment:

TIME:	EVENT:

For tomorrow:

_____
_____
_____
_____
_____

		1	2	3	4	5	6	7	8	9	10
IMPULSIVITY	Easily Frustrated	1	2	3	4	5	6	7	8	9	10
	Acting Without Thikining	1	2	3	4	5	6	7	8	9	10
	Interrupting Others	1	2	3	4	5	6	7	8	9	10
	Emotional Outbursts	1	2	3	4	5	6	7	8	9	10
HYPERACTIVITY	Difficulty Sleeping	1	2	3	4	5	6	7	8	9	10
	Constantly Moving	1	2	3	4	5	6	7	8	9	10
	Unable to Sit Still / Fidgeting	1	2	3	4	5	6	7	8	9	10
	Excessive Talking	1	2	3	4	5	6	7	8	9	10
INATTENTION	Easily Distracted	1	2	3	4	5	6	7	8	9	10
	Careless Mistakes	1	2	3	4	5	6	7	8	9	10
	Short Attention	1	2	3	4	5	6	7	8	9	10
	Forgetfulness	1	2	3	4	5	6	7	8	9	10

Date _____

DAILY PLANNER

TODAY'S GOALS

MOOD:

PRIORITIES WITH CONSEQUENCES

A

WATER INTAKE:

A

THINGS TO GET DONE TODAY:

TODAY'S APPOINTMENT:

A

TIME: EVENT:

FOR TOMORROW:

		1	2	3	4	5	6	7	8	9	10
IMPULSIVITY	Easily Frustrated	1	2	3	4	5	6	7	8	9	10
	Acting Without Thikining	1	2	3	4	5	6	7	8	9	10
	Interrupting Others	1	2	3	4	5	6	7	8	9	10
	Emotional Outbursts	1	2	3	4	5	6	7	8	9	10
HYPERACTIVITY	Difficulty Sleeping	1	2	3	4	5	6	7	8	9	10
	Constantly Moving	1	2	3	4	5	6	7	8	9	10
	Unable to Sit Still / Fidgeting	1	2	3	4	5	6	7	8	9	10
	Excessive Talking	1	2	3	4	5	6	7	8	9	10
INATTENTION	Easily Distracted	1	2	3	4	5	6	7	8	9	10
	Careless Mistakes	1	2	3	4	5	6	7	8	9	10
	Short Attention	1	2	3	4	5	6	7	8	9	10
	Forgetfulness	1	2	3	4	5	6	7	8	9	10

MEDICATION
Tracker

	MEDICATION	DOSAGE	FREQUENCY	TAKEN
MONDAY				
TUESDAY				
WEDNESDAY				
THURSDAY				
FRIDAY				
SATURDAY				
SUNDAY				

NOTES

Nothing like ADHD and a good
fight to the death to make time fly.

–Rick Riordan

TO DO'S
Weekly

Must Do!

_____

_____

_____

Important

- _____
- _____
- _____
- _____
- _____
- _____
- _____
- _____
- _____
- _____

Less important

- _____
- _____
- _____
- _____
- _____
- _____
- _____
- _____
- _____
- _____

Notes

_____   _____

_____   _____

_____   _____

_____   _____

HABIT TRACKER
Weekly

HÁBITS	MON	TUES	WED	THU	FRI	SAT	SUN
	○	○	○	○	○	○	○
	○	○	○	○	○	○	○
	○	○	○	○	○	○	○
	○	○	○	○	○	○	○
	○	○	○	○	○	○	○
	○	○	○	○	○	○	○
	○	○	○	○	○	○	○
	○	○	○	○	○	○	○
	○	○	○	○	○	○	○
	○	○	○	○	○	○	○
	○	○	○	○	○	○	○
	○	○	○	○	○	○	○
	○	○	○	○	○	○	○
	○	○	○	○	○	○	○

HOW DID I DO?

"I have more thoughts before breakfast
than most people have all day."
— UNKNOWN

BRAIN DUMP

Though Organizer

MUST DO	SHOULD DO

COULD START	MUST DO

DAILY PLANNER

Today's goals

Mood:

Water Intake:

Priorities with Consequences

A+

A+

A+

Things to get done today:

_____
_____
_____
_____
_____
_____
_____
_____
_____

Today's appointment:

TIME: EVENT:

For tomorrow:

_____
_____
_____
_____
_____
_____

			1	2	3	4	5	6	7	8	9	10
IMPULSIVITY	Easily Frustrated		1	2	3	4	5	6	7	8	9	10
	Acting Without Thikining		1	2	3	4	5	6	7	8	9	10
	Interrupting Others		1	2	3	4	5	6	7	8	9	10
	Emotional Outbursts		1	2	3	4	5	6	7	8	9	10
HYPERACTIVITY	Difficulty Sleeping		1	2	3	4	5	6	7	8	9	10
	Constantly Moving		1	2	3	4	5	6	7	8	9	10
	Unable to Sit Still / Fidgeting		1	2	3	4	5	6	7	8	9	10
	Excessive Talking		1	2	3	4	5	6	7	8	9	10
INATTENTION	Easily Distracted		1	2	3	4	5	6	7	8	9	10
	Careless Mistakes		1	2	3	4	5	6	7	8	9	10
	Short Attention		1	2	3	4	5	6	7	8	9	10
	Forgetfulness		1	2	3	4	5	6	7	8	9	10

Date _____

DAILY PLANNER

TODAY'S GOALS

MOOD:

PRIORITIES WITH CONSEQUENCES

WATER INTAKE:

THINGS TO GET DONE TODAY:

_____
_____
_____
_____
_____
_____
_____
_____

TODAY'S APPOINTMENT:

TIME: EVENT:

FOR TOMORROW:

_____
_____
_____
_____

		1	2	3	4	5	6	7	8	9	10
IMPULSIVITY	Easily Frustrated	1	2	3	4	5	6	7	8	9	10
	Acting Without Thikining	1	2	3	4	5	6	7	8	9	10
	Interrupting Others	1	2	3	4	5	6	7	8	9	10
	Emotional Outbursts	1	2	3	4	5	6	7	8	9	10
HYPERACTIVITY	Difficulty Sleeping	1	2	3	4	5	6	7	8	9	10
	Constantly Moving	1	2	3	4	5	6	7	8	9	10
	Unable to Sit Still / Fidgeting	1	2	3	4	5	6	7	8	9	10
	Excessive Talking	1	2	3	4	5	6	7	8	9	10
INATTENTION	Easily Distracted	1	2	3	4	5	6	7	8	9	10
	Careless Mistakes	1	2	3	4	5	6	7	8	9	10
	Short Attention	1	2	3	4	5	6	7	8	9	10
	Forgetfulness	1	2	3	4	5	6	7	8	9	10

DAILY PLANNER

TODAY'S GOALS

MOOD:

PRIORITIES WITH CONSEQUENCES

WATER INTAKE:

THINGS TO GET DONE TODAY:

_____
_____
_____
_____
_____
_____
_____
_____
_____

TODAY'S APPOINTMENT:

TIME:	EVENT:

FOR TOMORROW:

_____
_____
_____
_____
_____

		1	2	3	4	5	6	7	8	9	10
IMPULSIVITY	Easily Frustrated	1	2	3	4	5	6	7	8	9	10
	Acting Without Thikining	1	2	3	4	5	6	7	8	9	10
	Interrupting Others	1	2	3	4	5	6	7	8	9	10
	Emotional Outbursts	1	2	3	4	5	6	7	8	9	10
HYPERACTIVITY	Difficulty Sleeping	1	2	3	4	5	6	7	8	9	10
	Constantly Moving	1	2	3	4	5	6	7	8	9	10
	Unable to Sit Still / Fidgeting	1	2	3	4	5	6	7	8	9	10
	Excessive Talking	1	2	3	4	5	6	7	8	9	10
INATTENTION	Easily Distracted	1	2	3	4	5	6	7	8	9	10
	Careless Mistakes	1	2	3	4	5	6	7	8	9	10
	Short Attention	1	2	3	4	5	6	7	8	9	10
	Forgetfulness	1	2	3	4	5	6	7	8	9	10

DAILY PLANNER

Today's goals

Mood:

Water Intake:

Priorities with Consequences

A⁺

A⁺

A⁺

Things to get done today:

_____
_____
_____
_____
_____
_____
_____
_____

Today's appointment:

TIME:	EVENT:

For tomorrow:

_____
_____
_____
_____
_____

		1	2	3	4	5	6	7	8	9	10
IMPULSIVITY	Easily Frustrated	1	2	3	4	5	6	7	8	9	10
	Acting Without Thikining	1	2	3	4	5	6	7	8	9	10
	Interrupting Others	1	2	3	4	5	6	7	8	9	10
	Emotional Outbursts	1	2	3	4	5	6	7	8	9	10
HYPERACTIVITY	Difficulty Sleeping	1	2	3	4	5	6	7	8	9	10
	Constantly Moving	1	2	3	4	5	6	7	8	9	10
	Unable to Sit Still / Fidgeting	1	2	3	4	5	6	7	8	9	10
	Excessive Talking	1	2	3	4	5	6	7	8	9	10
INATTENTION	Easily Distracted	1	2	3	4	5	6	7	8	9	10
	Careless Mistakes	1	2	3	4	5	6	7	8	9	10
	Short Attention	1	2	3	4	5	6	7	8	9	10
	Forgetfulness	1	2	3	4	5	6	7	8	9	10

DAILY PLANNER

Today's goals

Mood:

Water Intake:

Priorities with Consequences

A⁺

A⁺

A⁺

Things to get done today:

_____
_____
_____
_____
_____
_____
_____
_____
_____

Today's appointment:

TIME:	EVENT:

For tomorrow:

_____
_____
_____
_____
_____

		1	2	3	4	5	6	7	8	9	10
IMPULSIVITY	Easily Frustrated	1	2	3	4	5	6	7	8	9	10
	Acting Without Thikining	1	2	3	4	5	6	7	8	9	10
	Interrupting Others	1	2	3	4	5	6	7	8	9	10
	Emotional Outbursts	1	2	3	4	5	6	7	8	9	10
HYPERACTIVITY	Difficulty Sleeping	1	2	3	4	5	6	7	8	9	10
	Constantly Moving	1	2	3	4	5	6	7	8	9	10
	Unable to Sit Still / Fidgeting	1	2	3	4	5	6	7	8	9	10
	Excessive Talking	1	2	3	4	5	6	7	8	9	10
INATTENTION	Easily Distracted	1	2	3	4	5	6	7	8	9	10
	Careless Mistakes	1	2	3	4	5	6	7	8	9	10
	Short Attention	1	2	3	4	5	6	7	8	9	10
	Forgetfulness	1	2	3	4	5	6	7	8	9	10

Date _____

DAILY PLANNER

Today's Goals

Mood:

Water Intake:

Priorities with Consequences

A⁺

A⁺

A⁺

Things to get done today:

_____
_____
_____
_____
_____
_____
_____
_____

Today's appointment:

TIME:	EVENT:

For tomorrow:

_____
_____
_____
_____
_____

		1	2	3	4	5	6	7	8	9	10
IMPULSIVITY	Easily Frustrated	1	2	3	4	5	6	7	8	9	10
	Acting Without Thikining	1	2	3	4	5	6	7	8	9	10
	Interrupting Others	1	2	3	4	5	6	7	8	9	10
	Emotional Outbursts	1	2	3	4	5	6	7	8	9	10
HYPERACTIVITY	Difficulty Sleeping	1	2	3	4	5	6	7	8	9	10
	Constantly Moving	1	2	3	4	5	6	7	8	9	10
	Unable to Sit Still / Fidgeting	1	2	3	4	5	6	7	8	9	10
	Excessive Talking	1	2	3	4	5	6	7	8	9	10
INATTENTION	Easily Distracted	1	2	3	4	5	6	7	8	9	10
	Careless Mistakes	1	2	3	4	5	6	7	8	9	10
	Short Attention	1	2	3	4	5	6	7	8	9	10
	Forgetfulness	1	2	3	4	5	6	7	8	9	10

DAILY PLANNER

Today's goals

Mood:

Water Intake:

Priorities with Consequences

A⁺

A⁺

A⁺

Things to get done today:

Today's appointment:

TIME: EVENT:

For tomorrow:

		1	2	3	4	5	6	7	8	9	10
IMPULSIVITY	Easily Frustrated	1	2	3	4	5	6	7	8	9	10
	Acting Without Thikining	1	2	3	4	5	6	7	8	9	10
	Interrupting Others	1	2	3	4	5	6	7	8	9	10
	Emotional Outbursts	1	2	3	4	5	6	7	8	9	10
HYPERACTIVITY	Difficulty Sleeping	1	2	3	4	5	6	7	8	9	10
	Constantly Moving	1	2	3	4	5	6	7	8	9	10
	Unable to Sit Still / Fidgeting	1	2	3	4	5	6	7	8	9	10
	Excessive Talking	1	2	3	4	5	6	7	8	9	10
INATTENTION	Easily Distracted	1	2	3	4	5	6	7	8	9	10
	Careless Mistakes	1	2	3	4	5	6	7	8	9	10
	Short Attention	1	2	3	4	5	6	7	8	9	10
	Forgetfulness	1	2	3	4	5	6	7	8	9	10

MEDICATION
Tracker

	MEDICATION	DOSAGE	FREQUENCY	TAKEN
MONDAY				
TUESDAY				
WEDNESDAY				
THURSDAY				
FRIDAY				
SATURDAY				
SUNDAY				

NOTES

Nothing like ADHD and a good
fight to the death to make time fly.

—RICK RIORDAN

TO DO'S
Weekly

MUST DO!

_____

_____

_____

IMPORTANT

_____

_____

_____

_____

_____

_____

_____

_____

_____

_____

LESS IMPORTANT

_____

_____

_____

_____

_____

_____

_____

_____

_____

_____

NOTES

_____

_____

_____

_____

_____

_____

In the power of fixing the attention lies the most precious of the intellectual habits.

— Robert Hall

HABIT TRACKER
Weekly

HÁBITS	MON	TUES	WED	THU	FRI	SAT	SUN
_____	○	○	○	○	○	○	○
_____	○	○	○	○	○	○	○
_____	○	○	○	○	○	○	○
_____	○	○	○	○	○	○	○
_____	○	○	○	○	○	○	○
_____	○	○	○	○	○	○	○
_____	○	○	○	○	○	○	○
_____	○	○	○	○	○	○	○
_____	○	○	○	○	○	○	○
_____	○	○	○	○	○	○	○
_____	○	○	○	○	○	○	○
_____	○	○	○	○	○	○	○
_____	○	○	○	○	○	○	○
_____	○	○	○	○	○	○	○

HOW DID I DO?

"I have more thoughts before breakfast
than most people have all day."
— UNKNOWN

BRAIN DUMP
Though Organizer

MUST DO	SHOULD DO

COULD START	MUST DO

DAILY PLANNER

Today's goals

Mood:

Water Intake:

Priorities with Consequences

A⁺

A⁺

A⁺

Things to get done today:

_____
_____
_____
_____
_____
_____
_____
_____
_____

Today's appointment:

TIME: **EVENT:**

For tomorrow:

_____
_____
_____
_____
_____

		1	2	3	4	5	6	7	8	9	10
IMPULSIVITY	Easily Frustrated	1	2	3	4	5	6	7	8	9	10
	Acting Without Thikining	1	2	3	4	5	6	7	8	9	10
	Interrupting Others	1	2	3	4	5	6	7	8	9	10
	Emotional Outbursts	1	2	3	4	5	6	7	8	9	10
HYPERACTIVITY	Difficulty Sleeping	1	2	3	4	5	6	7	8	9	10
	Constantly Moving	1	2	3	4	5	6	7	8	9	10
	Unable to Sit Still / Fidgeting	1	2	3	4	5	6	7	8	9	10
	Excessive Talking	1	2	3	4	5	6	7	8	9	10
INATTENTION	Easily Distracted	1	2	3	4	5	6	7	8	9	10
	Careless Mistakes	1	2	3	4	5	6	7	8	9	10
	Short Attention	1	2	3	4	5	6	7	8	9	10
	Forgetfulness	1	2	3	4	5	6	7	8	9	10

Date _____

DAILY PLANNER

TODAY'S GOALS

MOOD:

PRIORITIES WITH CONSEQUENCES

A⁺

WATER INTAKE:

A⁺

THINGS TO GET DONE TODAY:

_____
_____
_____
_____
_____
_____
_____
_____

TODAY'S APPOINTMENT:

TIME:	EVENT:

A⁺

FOR TOMORROW:

_____
_____
_____
_____
_____

		1	2	3	4	5	6	7	8	9	10
IMPULSIVITY	Easily Frustrated	1	2	3	4	5	6	7	8	9	10
	Acting Without Thikining	1	2	3	4	5	6	7	8	9	10
	Interrupting Others	1	2	3	4	5	6	7	8	9	10
	Emotional Outbursts	1	2	3	4	5	6	7	8	9	10
HYPERACTIVITY	Difficulty Sleeping	1	2	3	4	5	6	7	8	9	10
	Constantly Moving	1	2	3	4	5	6	7	8	9	10
	Unable to Sit Still / Fidgeting	1	2	3	4	5	6	7	8	9	10
	Excessive Talking	1	2	3	4	5	6	7	8	9	10
INATTENTION	Easily Distracted	1	2	3	4	5	6	7	8	9	10
	Careless Mistakes	1	2	3	4	5	6	7	8	9	10
	Short Attention	1	2	3	4	5	6	7	8	9	10
	Forgetfulness	1	2	3	4	5	6	7	8	9	10

DAILY PLANNER

TODAY'S GOALS

MOOD:

WATER INTAKE:

PRIORITIES WITH CONSEQUENCES

A+

A+

THINGS TO GET DONE TODAY:

_____
_____
_____
_____
_____
_____
_____
_____

TODAY'S APPOINTMENT:

TIME:	EVENT:

A+

FOR TOMORROW:

_____
_____
_____
_____
_____

		1	2	3	4	5	6	7	8	9	10
IMPULSIVITY	Easily Frustrated	1	2	3	4	5	6	7	8	9	10
	Acting Without Thikining	1	2	3	4	5	6	7	8	9	10
	Interrupting Others	1	2	3	4	5	6	7	8	9	10
	Emotional Outbursts	1	2	3	4	5	6	7	8	9	10
HYPERACTIVITY	Difficulty Sleeping	1	2	3	4	5	6	7	8	9	10
	Constantly Moving	1	2	3	4	5	6	7	8	9	10
	Unable to Sit Still / Fidgeting	1	2	3	4	5	6	7	8	9	10
	Excessive Talking	1	2	3	4	5	6	7	8	9	10
INAITTENTION	Easily Distracted	1	2	3	4	5	6	7	8	9	10
	Careless Mistakes	1	2	3	4	5	6	7	8	9	10
	Short Attention	1	2	3	4	5	6	7	8	9	10
	Forgetfulness	1	2	3	4	5	6	7	8	9	10

DAILY PLANNER

Today's Goals

Mood:

Water Intake:

Priorities with Consequences

A⁺

A⁺

A⁺

Things to get done today:

_____
_____
_____
_____
_____
_____
_____
_____
_____

Today's appointment:

TIME:	EVENT:

For tomorrow:

_____
_____
_____
_____
_____
_____

		1	2	3	4	5	6	7	8	9	10
IMPULSIVITY	Easily Frustrated	1	2	3	4	5	6	7	8	9	10
	Acting Without Thikining	1	2	3	4	5	6	7	8	9	10
	Interrupting Others	1	2	3	4	5	6	7	8	9	10
	Emotional Outbursts	1	2	3	4	5	6	7	8	9	10
HYPERACTIVITY	Difficulty Sleeping	1	2	3	4	5	6	7	8	9	10
	Constantly Moving	1	2	3	4	5	6	7	8	9	10
	Unable to Sit Still / Fidgeting	1	2	3	4	5	6	7	8	9	10
	Excessive Talking	1	2	3	4	5	6	7	8	9	10
INATTENTION	Easily Distracted	1	2	3	4	5	6	7	8	9	10
	Careless Mistakes	1	2	3	4	5	6	7	8	9	10
	Short Attention	1	2	3	4	5	6	7	8	9	10
	Forgetfulness	1	2	3	4	5	6	7	8	9	10

DAILY PLANNER

Today's goals

Mood:

Water Intake:

Priorities with Consequences

A⁺

A⁺

A⁺

Things to get done today:

Today's appointment:

TIME:	EVENT:

For tomorrow:

		1	2	3	4	5	6	7	8	9	10
IMPULSIVITY	Easily Frustrated	1	2	3	4	5	6	7	8	9	10
	Acting Without Thikining	1	2	3	4	5	6	7	8	9	10
	Interrupting Others	1	2	3	4	5	6	7	8	9	10
	Emotional Outbursts	1	2	3	4	5	6	7	8	9	10
HYPERACTIVITY	Difficulty Sleeping	1	2	3	4	5	6	7	8	9	10
	Constantly Moving	1	2	3	4	5	6	7	8	9	10
	Unable to Sit Still / Fidgeting	1	2	3	4	5	6	7	8	9	10
	Excessive Talking	1	2	3	4	5	6	7	8	9	10
INATTENTION	Easily Distracted	1	2	3	4	5	6	7	8	9	10
	Careless Mistakes	1	2	3	4	5	6	7	8	9	10
	Short Attention	1	2	3	4	5	6	7	8	9	10
	Forgetfulness	1	2	3	4	5	6	7	8	9	10

Date _____

DAILY PLANNER

Today's Goals

Mood:

😊 🙂 😐 🙁 😢

Water Intake:

💧 💧 💧 💧 💧 💧 💧

Priorities with Consequences

A⁺

A⁺

A⁺

Things to get done today:

_____
_____
_____
_____
_____
_____
_____
_____

Today's appointment:

TIME:	EVENT:

For tomorrow:

_____
_____
_____
_____
_____

		1	2	3	4	5	6	7	8	9	10
IMPULSIVITY	Easily Frustrated	1	2	3	4	5	6	7	8	9	10
	Acting Without Thikining	1	2	3	4	5	6	7	8	9	10
	Interrupting Others	1	2	3	4	5	6	7	8	9	10
	Emotional Outbursts	1	2	3	4	5	6	7	8	9	10
HYPERACTIVITY	Difficulty Sleeping	1	2	3	4	5	6	7	8	9	10
	Constantly Moving	1	2	3	4	5	6	7	8	9	10
	Unable to Sit Still / Fidgeting	1	2	3	4	5	6	7	8	9	10
	Excessive Talking	1	2	3	4	5	6	7	8	9	10
INATTENTION	Easily Distracted	1	2	3	4	5	6	7	8	9	10
	Careless Mistakes	1	2	3	4	5	6	7	8	9	10
	Short Attention	1	2	3	4	5	6	7	8	9	10
	Forgetfulness	1	2	3	4	5	6	7	8	9	10

Date _____

DAILY PLANNER

Today's goals

Mood:
🙂 🙂 😐 🙁 ☹️

Water Intake:
💧💧💧💧💧💧💧

Priorities with Consequences

A⁺

A⁺

A⁺

Things to get done today:
_____
_____
_____
_____
_____
_____
_____
_____
_____

Today's appointment:

TIME:	EVENT:

For tomorrow:
_____
_____
_____
_____
_____

		1	2	3	4	5	6	7	8	9	10
IMPULSIVITY	Easily Frustrated	1	2	3	4	5	6	7	8	9	10
	Acting Without Thinking	1	2	3	4	5	6	7	8	9	10
	Interrupting Others	1	2	3	4	5	6	7	8	9	10
	Emotional Outbursts	1	2	3	4	5	6	7	8	9	10
HYPERACTIVITY	Difficulty Sleeping	1	2	3	4	5	6	7	8	9	10
	Constantly Moving	1	2	3	4	5	6	7	8	9	10
	Unable to Sit Still / Fidgeting	1	2	3	4	5	6	7	8	9	10
	Excessive Talking	1	2	3	4	5	6	7	8	9	10
INATTENTION	Easily Distracted	1	2	3	4	5	6	7	8	9	10
	Careless Mistakes	1	2	3	4	5	6	7	8	9	10
	Short Attention	1	2	3	4	5	6	7	8	9	10
	Forgetfulness	1	2	3	4	5	6	7	8	9	10

MEDICATION
Tracker

	MEDICATION	DOSAGE	FREQUENCY	TAKEN
MONDAY				
TUESDAY				
WEDNESDAY				
THURSDAY				
FRIDAY				
SATURDAY				
SUNDAY				

NOTES

Nothing like ADHD and a good
fight to the death to make time fly.

—RICK RIORDAN

TO DO'S
Weekly

MUST DO!

_____
_____
_____

IMPORTANT

_____
_____
_____
_____
_____
_____
_____
_____
_____
_____

LESS IMPORTANT

_____
_____
_____
_____
_____
_____
_____
_____
_____
_____

NOTES

_____   _____
_____   _____
_____   _____
_____   _____

In the power of fixing the attention lies the
most precious of the intellectual habits.
– ROBERT HALL

HABIT TRACKER
Weekly

HÁBITS	MON	TUES	WED	THU	FRI	SAT	SUN
	○	○	○	○	○	○	○
	○	○	○	○	○	○	○
	○	○	○	○	○	○	○
	○	○	○	○	○	○	○
	○	○	○	○	○	○	○
	○	○	○	○	○	○	○
	○	○	○	○	○	○	○
	○	○	○	○	○	○	○
	○	○	○	○	○	○	○
	○	○	○	○	○	○	○
	○	○	○	○	○	○	○
	○	○	○	○	○	○	○
	○	○	○	○	○	○	○
	○	○	○	○	○	○	○

HOW DID I DO?

"I have more thoughts before breakfast
than most people have all day."
— UNKNOWN

BRAIN DUMP
Though Organizer

MUST DO	SHOULD DO

COULD START	MUST DO

DAILY PLANNER

⊙ Today's goals

Mood:

😊 🙂 😐 🙁 ☹️

Water Intake:

◇◇◇◇◇◇◇◇

Priorities with Consequences

A⁺

A⁺

A⁺

Things to get done today:

_____
_____
_____
_____
_____
_____
_____
_____
_____
_____

Today's appointment:

TIME:	EVENT:

For tomorrow:

_____
_____
_____
_____
_____

		1	2	3	4	5	6	7	8	9	10
Impulsivity	Easily Frustrated	1	2	3	4	5	6	7	8	9	10
	Acting Without Thikining	1	2	3	4	5	6	7	8	9	10
	Interrupting Others	1	2	3	4	5	6	7	8	9	10
	Emotional Outbursts	1	2	3	4	5	6	7	8	9	10
Hyperactivity	Difficulty Sleeping	1	2	3	4	5	6	7	8	9	10
	Constantly Moving	1	2	3	4	5	6	7	8	9	10
	Unable to Sit Still / Fidgeting	1	2	3	4	5	6	7	8	9	10
	Excessive Talking	1	2	3	4	5	6	7	8	9	10
Inatention	Easily Distracted	1	2	3	4	5	6	7	8	9	10
	Careless Mistakes	1	2	3	4	5	6	7	8	9	10
	Short Attention	1	2	3	4	5	6	7	8	9	10
	Forgetfulness	1	2	3	4	5	6	7	8	9	10

Date _____

DAILY PLANNER

TODAY'S GOALS

MOOD:

😄 🙂 😐 🙁 😢

WATER INTAKE:

💧💧💧💧💧💧💧

PRIORITIES WITH CONSEQUENCES

A⁺

A⁺

A⁺

THINGS TO GET DONE TODAY:

_____
_____
_____
_____
_____
_____
_____
_____

TODAY'S APPOINTMENT:

TIME:	EVENT:

FOR TOMORROW:

_____
_____
_____
_____

		1	2	3	4	5	6	7	8	9	10
IMPULSIVITY	Easily Frustrated	1	2	3	4	5	6	7	8	9	10
	Acting Without Thikining	1	2	3	4	5	6	7	8	9	10
	Interrupting Others	1	2	3	4	5	6	7	8	9	10
	Emotional Outbursts	1	2	3	4	5	6	7	8	9	10
HYPERACTIVITY	Difficulty Sleeping	1	2	3	4	5	6	7	8	9	10
	Constantly Moving	1	2	3	4	5	6	7	8	9	10
	Unable to Sit Still / Fidgeting	1	2	3	4	5	6	7	8	9	10
	Excessive Talking	1	2	3	4	5	6	7	8	9	10
INATTENTION	Easily Distracted	1	2	3	4	5	6	7	8	9	10
	Careless Mistakes	1	2	3	4	5	6	7	8	9	10
	Short Attention	1	2	3	4	5	6	7	8	9	10
	Forgetfulness	1	2	3	4	5	6	7	8	9	10

Date _____

DAILY PLANNER

Today's goals

Mood:

😄 🙂 😐 🙁 😣

Water Intake:

💧💧💧💧💧💧💧💧

Priorities with Consequences

A⁺

A⁺

Things to get done today:

_____
_____
_____
_____
_____
_____
_____
_____
_____
_____

Today's appointment:

TIME:	EVENT:

A⁺

For tomorrow:

_____
_____
_____
_____
_____

		1	2	3	4	5	6	7	8	9	10
IMPULSIVITY	Easily Frustrated	1	2	3	4	5	6	7	8	9	10
	Acting Without Thikining	1	2	3	4	5	6	7	8	9	10
	Interrupting Others	1	2	3	4	5	6	7	8	9	10
	Emotional Outbursts	1	2	3	4	5	6	7	8	9	10
HYPERACTIVITY	Difficulty Sleeping	1	2	3	4	5	6	7	8	9	10
	Constantly Moving	1	2	3	4	5	6	7	8	9	10
	Unable to Sit Still / Fidgeting	1	2	3	4	5	6	7	8	9	10
	Excessive Talking	1	2	3	4	5	6	7	8	9	10
INATTENTION	Easily Distracted	1	2	3	4	5	6	7	8	9	10
	Careless Mistakes	1	2	3	4	5	6	7	8	9	10
	Short Attention	1	2	3	4	5	6	7	8	9	10
	Forgetfulness	1	2	3	4	5	6	7	8	9	10

Date _____

DAILY PLANNER

TODAY'S GOALS

MOOD:

PRIORITIES WITH CONSEQUENCES

WATER INTAKE:

THINGS TO GET DONE TODAY:

TODAY'S APPOINTMENT:

TIME: EVENT:

FOR TOMORROW:

		1	2	3	4	5	6	7	8	9	10
IMPULSIVITY	Easily Frustrated	1	2	3	4	5	6	7	8	9	10
	Acting Without Thikining	1	2	3	4	5	6	7	8	9	10
	Interrupting Others	1	2	3	4	5	6	7	8	9	10
	Emotional Outbursts	1	2	3	4	5	6	7	8	9	10
HYPERACTIVITY	Difficulty Sleeping	1	2	3	4	5	6	7	8	9	10
	Constantly Moving	1	2	3	4	5	6	7	8	9	10
	Unable to Sit Still / Fidgeting	1	2	3	4	5	6	7	8	9	10
	Excessive Talking	1	2	3	4	5	6	7	8	9	10
INATTENTION	Easily Distracted	1	2	3	4	5	6	7	8	9	10
	Careless Mistakes	1	2	3	4	5	6	7	8	9	10
	Short Attention	1	2	3	4	5	6	7	8	9	10
	Forgetfulness	1	2	3	4	5	6	7	8	9	10

Date _____

DAILY PLANNER

Today's goals

Mood:

😄 🙂 😐 🙁 ☹️

Water Intake:

💧💧💧💧💧💧💧💧

Priorities with Consequences

A⁺

A⁺

A⁺

Things to get done today:

_____
_____
_____
_____
_____
_____
_____
_____
_____
_____

Today's appointment:

TIME: EVENT:

_____
_____
_____
_____
_____
_____
_____
_____

For tomorrow:

_____
_____
_____
_____
_____

		1	2	3	4	5	6	7	8	9	10
IMPULSIVITY	Easily Frustrated	1	2	3	4	5	6	7	8	9	10
	Acting Without Thikining	1	2	3	4	5	6	7	8	9	10
	Interrupting Others	1	2	3	4	5	6	7	8	9	10
	Emotional Outbursts	1	2	3	4	5	6	7	8	9	10
HYPERACTIVITY	Difficulty Sleeping	1	2	3	4	5	6	7	8	9	10
	Constantly Moving	1	2	3	4	5	6	7	8	9	10
	Unable to Sit Still / Fidgeting	1	2	3	4	5	6	7	8	9	10
	Excessive Talking	1	2	3	4	5	6	7	8	9	10
INATTENTION	Easily Distracted	1	2	3	4	5	6	7	8	9	10
	Careless Mistakes	1	2	3	4	5	6	7	8	9	10
	Short Attention	1	2	3	4	5	6	7	8	9	10
	Forgetfulness	1	2	3	4	5	6	7	8	9	10

DAILY PLANNER

Today's goals

Mood:

Water Intake:

Priorities with Consequences

A⁺

A⁺

A⁺

Things to get done today:

_____
_____
_____
_____
_____
_____
_____
_____
_____

Today's appointment:

TIME: EVENT:

For tomorrow:

_____
_____
_____
_____
_____

		1	2	3	4	5	6	7	8	9	10
IMPULSIVITY	Easily Frustrated	1	2	3	4	5	6	7	8	9	10
	Acting Without Thikining	1	2	3	4	5	6	7	8	9	10
	Interrupting Others	1	2	3	4	5	6	7	8	9	10
	Emotional Outbursts	1	2	3	4	5	6	7	8	9	10
HYPERACTIVITY	Difficulty Sleeping	1	2	3	4	5	6	7	8	9	10
	Constantly Moving	1	2	3	4	5	6	7	8	9	10
	Unable to Sit Still / Fidgeting	1	2	3	4	5	6	7	8	9	10
	Excessive Talking	1	2	3	4	5	6	7	8	9	10
INATTENTION	Easily Distracted	1	2	3	4	5	6	7	8	9	10
	Careless Mistakes	1	2	3	4	5	6	7	8	9	10
	Short Attention	1	2	3	4	5	6	7	8	9	10
	Forgetfulness	1	2	3	4	5	6	7	8	9	10

Date _____

DAILY PLANNER

TODAY'S GOALS

MOOD:

PRIORITIES WITH CONSEQUENCES

A⁺

WATER INTAKE:

A⁺

THINGS TO GET DONE TODAY:

TODAY'S APPOINTMENT:

A⁺

_____
_____
_____
_____
_____
_____
_____
_____
_____

TIME:	EVENT:

FOR TOMORROW:

_____
_____
_____
_____
_____

		1	2	3	4	5	6	7	8	9	10
IMPULSIVITY	Easily Frustrated	1	2	3	4	5	6	7	8	9	10
	Acting Without Thikining	1	2	3	4	5	6	7	8	9	10
	Interrupting Others	1	2	3	4	5	6	7	8	9	10
	Emotional Outbursts	1	2	3	4	5	6	7	8	9	10
HYPERACTIVITY	Difficulty Sleeping	1	2	3	4	5	6	7	8	9	10
	Constantly Moving	1	2	3	4	5	6	7	8	9	10
	Unable to Sit Still / Fidgeting	1	2	3	4	5	6	7	8	9	10
	Excessive Talking	1	2	3	4	5	6	7	8	9	10
INATTENTION	Easily Distracted	1	2	3	4	5	6	7	8	9	10
	Careless Mistakes	1	2	3	4	5	6	7	8	9	10
	Short Attention	1	2	3	4	5	6	7	8	9	10
	Forgetfulness	1	2	3	4	5	6	7	8	9	10

MEDICATION
Tracker

	MEDICATION	DOSAGE	FREQUENCY	TAKEN
MONDAY				
TUESDAY				
WEDNESDAY				
THURSDAY				
FRIDAY				
SATURDAY				
SUNDAY				

NOTES

Nothing like ADHD and a good
fight to the death to make time fly.

—RICK RIORDAN

TO DO'S
Weekly

MUST DO!

_____

_____

_____

IMPORTANT

- _____
- _____
- _____
- _____
- _____
- _____
- _____
- _____
- _____

LESS IMPORTANT

- _____
- _____
- _____
- _____
- _____
- _____
- _____
- _____
- _____

NOTES

_____   _____

_____   _____

_____   _____

_____   _____

HABIT TRACKER
Weekly

HÁBITS	MON	TUES	WED	THU	FRI	SAT	SUN
_____	◯	◯	◯	◯	◯	◯	◯
_____	◯	◯	◯	◯	◯	◯	◯
_____	◯	◯	◯	◯	◯	◯	◯
_____	◯	◯	◯	◯	◯	◯	◯
_____	◯	◯	◯	◯	◯	◯	◯
_____	◯	◯	◯	◯	◯	◯	◯
_____	◯	◯	◯	◯	◯	◯	◯
_____	◯	◯	◯	◯	◯	◯	◯
_____	◯	◯	◯	◯	◯	◯	◯
_____	◯	◯	◯	◯	◯	◯	◯
_____	◯	◯	◯	◯	◯	◯	◯
_____	◯	◯	◯	◯	◯	◯	◯
_____	◯	◯	◯	◯	◯	◯	◯
_____	◯	◯	◯	◯	◯	◯	◯

HOW DID I DO?

"I have more thoughts before breakfast
than most people have all day."
— UNKNOWN

BRAIN DUMP

Though Organizer

MUST DO	SHOULD DO

COULD START	MUST DO

DAILY PLANNER

Today's goals

Mood:

Priorities with Consequences

A⁺

Water Intake:

A⁺

Things to get done today:

Today's appointment:

A⁺

TIME:	EVENT:

For tomorrow:

		1	2	3	4	5	6	7	8	9	10
IMPULSIVITY	Easily Frustrated	1	2	3	4	5	6	7	8	9	10
	Acting Without Thikining	1	2	3	4	5	6	7	8	9	10
	Interrupting Others	1	2	3	4	5	6	7	8	9	10
	Emotional Outbursts	1	2	3	4	5	6	7	8	9	10
HYPERACTIVITY	Difficulty Sleeping	1	2	3	4	5	6	7	8	9	10
	Constantly Moving	1	2	3	4	5	6	7	8	9	10
	Unable to Sit Still / Fidgeting	1	2	3	4	5	6	7	8	9	10
	Excessive Talking	1	2	3	4	5	6	7	8	9	10
INATTENTION	Easily Distracted	1	2	3	4	5	6	7	8	9	10
	Careless Mistakes	1	2	3	4	5	6	7	8	9	10
	Short Attention	1	2	3	4	5	6	7	8	9	10
	Forgetfulness	1	2	3	4	5	6	7	8	9	10

Date _____

DAILY PLANNER

TODAY'S GOALS

MOOD:

WATER INTAKE:

THINGS TO GET DONE TODAY:

_____
_____
_____
_____
_____
_____
_____
_____

TODAY'S APPOINTMENT:

TIME:	EVENT:

PRIORITIES WITH CONSEQUENCES

A⁺

A⁺

A⁺

FOR TOMORROW:

_____
_____
_____
_____
_____

		1	2	3	4	5	6	7	8	9	10
IMPULSIVITY	Easily Frustrated	1	2	3	4	5	6	7	8	9	10
	Acting Without Thikining	1	2	3	4	5	6	7	8	9	10
	Interrupting Others	1	2	3	4	5	6	7	8	9	10
	Emotional Outbursts	1	2	3	4	5	6	7	8	9	10
HYPERACTIVITY	Difficulty Sleeping	1	2	3	4	5	6	7	8	9	10
	Constantly Moving	1	2	3	4	5	6	7	8	9	10
	Unable to Sit Still / Fidgeting	1	2	3	4	5	6	7	8	9	10
	Excessive Talking	1	2	3	4	5	6	7	8	9	10
INATTENTION	Easily Distracted	1	2	3	4	5	6	7	8	9	10
	Careless Mistakes	1	2	3	4	5	6	7	8	9	10
	Short Attention	1	2	3	4	5	6	7	8	9	10
	Forgetfulness	1	2	3	4	5	6	7	8	9	10

Date _____

DAILY PLANNER

Today's goals

Mood:
☺ ☺ ☺ ☹ ☹

Water Intake:
◇ ◇ ◇ ◇ ◇ ◇ ◇ ◇

Priorities with Consequences

A⁺

A⁺

A⁺

Things to get done today:

_____
_____
_____
_____
_____
_____
_____
_____

Today's appointment:

TIME:	EVENT:

For tomorrow:

_____
_____
_____
_____
_____

		1	2	3	4	5	6	7	8	9	10
IMPULSIVITY	Easily Frustrated	1	2	3	4	5	6	7	8	9	10
	Acting Without Thikining	1	2	3	4	5	6	7	8	9	10
	Interrupting Others	1	2	3	4	5	6	7	8	9	10
	Emotional Outbursts	1	2	3	4	5	6	7	8	9	10
HYPERACTIVITY	Difficulty Sleeping	1	2	3	4	5	6	7	8	9	10
	Constantly Moving	1	2	3	4	5	6	7	8	9	10
	Unable to Sit Still / Fidgeting	1	2	3	4	5	6	7	8	9	10
	Excessive Talking	1	2	3	4	5	6	7	8	9	10
INATTENTION	Easily Distracted	1	2	3	4	5	6	7	8	9	10
	Careless Mistakes	1	2	3	4	5	6	7	8	9	10
	Short Attention	1	2	3	4	5	6	7	8	9	10
	Forgetfulness	1	2	3	4	5	6	7	8	9	10

 Date _____

DAILY PLANNER

Today's goals

Mood:

😄 🙂 😐 🙁 😫

Water Intake:

💧💧💧💧💧💧💧💧

Priorities with Consequences

A⁺

A⁺

A⁺

Things to get done today:

_____
_____
_____
_____
_____
_____
_____
_____

Today's appointment:

TIME:	EVENT:

For tomorrow:

_____
_____
_____
_____
_____

		1	2	3	4	5	6	7	8	9	10
IMPULSIVITY	Easily Frustrated	1	2	3	4	5	6	7	8	9	10
	Acting Without Thikining	1	2	3	4	5	6	7	8	9	10
	Interrupting Others	1	2	3	4	5	6	7	8	9	10
	Emotional Outbursts	1	2	3	4	5	6	7	8	9	10
HYPERACTIVITY	Difficulty Sleeping	1	2	3	4	5	6	7	8	9	10
	Constantly Moving	1	2	3	4	5	6	7	8	9	10
	Unable to Sit Still / Fidgeting	1	2	3	4	5	6	7	8	9	10
	Excessive Talking	1	2	3	4	5	6	7	8	9	10
INATTENTION	Easily Distracted	1	2	3	4	5	6	7	8	9	10
	Careless Mistakes	1	2	3	4	5	6	7	8	9	10
	Short Attention	1	2	3	4	5	6	7	8	9	10
	Forgetfulness	1	2	3	4	5	6	7	8	9	10

Date _____

DAILY PLANNER

TODAY'S GOALS

MOOD:

😄 🙂 😐 🙁 ☹️

PRIORITIES WITH CONSEQUENCES

A⁺

WATER INTAKE:

💧 💧 💧 💧 💧 💧 💧

A⁺

THINGS TO GET DONE TODAY:

_____
_____
_____
_____
_____
_____
_____
_____
_____
_____

TODAY'S APPOINTMENT:

A⁺

TIME:	EVENT:

FOR TOMORROW:

_____
_____
_____
_____
_____
_____

		1	2	3	4	5	6	7	8	9	10
IMPULSIVITY	Easily Frustrated	1	2	3	4	5	6	7	8	9	10
	Acting Without Thikining	1	2	3	4	5	6	7	8	9	10
	Interrupting Others	1	2	3	4	5	6	7	8	9	10
	Emotional Outbursts	1	2	3	4	5	6	7	8	9	10
HYPERACTIVITY	Difficulty Sleeping	1	2	3	4	5	6	7	8	9	10
	Constantly Moving	1	2	3	4	5	6	7	8	9	10
	Unable to Sit Still / Fidgeting	1	2	3	4	5	6	7	8	9	10
	Excessive Talking	1	2	3	4	5	6	7	8	9	10
INATTENTION	Easily Distracted	1	2	3	4	5	6	7	8	9	10
	Careless Mistakes	1	2	3	4	5	6	7	8	9	10
	Short Attention	1	2	3	4	5	6	7	8	9	10
	Forgetfulness	1	2	3	4	5	6	7	8	9	10

DAILY PLANNER

🎯 TODAY'S GOALS

MOOD:

😊 🙂 😐 🙁 😢

WATER INTAKE:

💧💧💧💧💧💧💧

PRIORITIES WITH CONSEQUENCES

A⁺

A⁺

THINGS TO GET DONE TODAY:

_____
_____
_____
_____
_____
_____
_____
_____

TODAY'S APPOINTMENT:

TIME:	EVENT:

A⁺

FOR TOMORROW:

_____
_____
_____
_____
_____

		1	2	3	4	5	6	7	8	9	10
IMPULSIVITY	Easily Frustrated	1	2	3	4	5	6	7	8	9	10
	Acting Without Thikining	1	2	3	4	5	6	7	8	9	10
	Interrupting Others	1	2	3	4	5	6	7	8	9	10
	Emotional Outbursts	1	2	3	4	5	6	7	8	9	10
HYPERACTIVITY	Difficulty Sleeping	1	2	3	4	5	6	7	8	9	10
	Constantly Moving	1	2	3	4	5	6	7	8	9	10
	Unable to Sit Still / Fidgeting	1	2	3	4	5	6	7	8	9	10
	Excessive Talking	1	2	3	4	5	6	7	8	9	10
INATTENTION	Easily Distracted	1	2	3	4	5	6	7	8	9	10
	Careless Mistakes	1	2	3	4	5	6	7	8	9	10
	Short Attention	1	2	3	4	5	6	7	8	9	10
	Forgetfulness	1	2	3	4	5	6	7	8	9	10

DAILY PLANNER

Today's Goals

Mood:

😄 🙂 😐 🙁 ☹️

Priorities with Consequences

A^+

Water Intake:

A^+

Things to get done today:

_____
_____
_____
_____
_____
_____
_____
_____

Today's appointment:

TIME:	EVENT:

A^+

For tomorrow:

_____
_____
_____
_____
_____

		1	2	3	4	5	6	7	8	9	10
IMPULSIVITY	Easily Frustrated	1	2	3	4	5	6	7	8	9	10
	Acting Without Thikining	1	2	3	4	5	6	7	8	9	10
	Interrupting Others	1	2	3	4	5	6	7	8	9	10
	Emotional Outbursts	1	2	3	4	5	6	7	8	9	10
HYPERACTIVITY	Difficulty Sleeping	1	2	3	4	5	6	7	8	9	10
	Constantly Moving	1	2	3	4	5	6	7	8	9	10
	Unable to Sit Still / Fidgeting	1	2	3	4	5	6	7	8	9	10
	Excessive Talking	1	2	3	4	5	6	7	8	9	10
INATTENTION	Easily Distracted	1	2	3	4	5	6	7	8	9	10
	Careless Mistakes	1	2	3	4	5	6	7	8	9	10
	Short Attention	1	2	3	4	5	6	7	8	9	10
	Forgetfulness	1	2	3	4	5	6	7	8	9	10

MEDICATION
Tracker

	MEDICATION	DOSAGE	FREQUENCY	TAKEN
MONDAY				
TUESDAY				
WEDNESDAY				
THURSDAY				
FRIDAY				
SATURDAY				
SUNDAY				

NOTES

Nothing like ADHD and a good
fight to the death to make time fly.

—RICK RIORDAN

TO DO'S
Weekly

MUST DO!

_____

_____

_____

IMPORTANT

- _____
- _____
- _____
- _____
- _____
- _____
- _____
- _____
- _____
- _____

LESS IMPORTANT

- _____
- _____
- _____
- _____
- _____
- _____
- _____
- _____
- _____
- _____

NOTES

_____   _____
_____   _____
_____   _____
_____   _____

HABIT TRACKER
Weekly

HÁBITS	MON	TUES	WED	THU	FRI	SAT	SUN
	○	○	○	○	○	○	○
	○	○	○	○	○	○	○
	○	○	○	○	○	○	○
	○	○	○	○	○	○	○
	○	○	○	○	○	○	○
	○	○	○	○	○	○	○
	○	○	○	○	○	○	○
	○	○	○	○	○	○	○
	○	○	○	○	○	○	○
	○	○	○	○	○	○	○
	○	○	○	○	○	○	○
	○	○	○	○	○	○	○
	○	○	○	○	○	○	○
	○	○	○	○	○	○	○

HOW DID I DO?

BRAIN DUMP

Though Organizer

MUST DO	SHOULD DO

COULD START	MUST DO

DAILY PLANNER

Today's goals

Mood:

Water Intake:

Priorities with Consequences

A⁺

A⁺

A⁺

Things to get done today:

_____
_____
_____
_____
_____
_____
_____
_____

Today's appointment:

TIME:	EVENT:

For tomorrow:

_____
_____
_____
_____
_____

		1	2	3	4	5	6	7	8	9	10
IMPULSIVITY	Easily Frustrated	1	2	3	4	5	6	7	8	9	10
	Acting Without Thikining	1	2	3	4	5	6	7	8	9	10
	Interrupting Others	1	2	3	4	5	6	7	8	9	10
	Emotional Outbursts	1	2	3	4	5	6	7	8	9	10
HYPERACTIVITY	Difficulty Sleeping	1	2	3	4	5	6	7	8	9	10
	Constantly Moving	1	2	3	4	5	6	7	8	9	10
	Unable to Sit Still / Fidgeting	1	2	3	4	5	6	7	8	9	10
	Excessive Talking	1	2	3	4	5	6	7	8	9	10
INATTENTION	Easily Distracted	1	2	3	4	5	6	7	8	9	10
	Careless Mistakes	1	2	3	4	5	6	7	8	9	10
	Short Attention	1	2	3	4	5	6	7	8	9	10
	Forgetfulness	1	2	3	4	5	6	7	8	9	10

 Date _____

DAILY PLANNER

Today's Goals

Mood:

Priorities with Consequences

A⁺

A⁺

Water Intake:

A⁺

Things to get done today:

_____
_____
_____
_____
_____
_____
_____
_____

Today's appointment:

TIME:	EVENT:

For tomorrow:

_____
_____
_____
_____

		1	2	3	4	5	6	7	8	9	10
IMPULSIVITY	Easily Frustrated	1	2	3	4	5	6	7	8	9	10
	Acting Without Thiking	1	2	3	4	5	6	7	8	9	10
	Interrupting Others	1	2	3	4	5	6	7	8	9	10
	Emotional Outbursts	1	2	3	4	5	6	7	8	9	10
HYPERACTIVITY	Difficulty Sleeping	1	2	3	4	5	6	7	8	9	10
	Constantly Moving	1	2	3	4	5	6	7	8	9	10
	Unable to Sit Still / Fidgeting	1	2	3	4	5	6	7	8	9	10
	Excessive Talking	1	2	3	4	5	6	7	8	9	10
INATTENTION	Easily Distracted	1	2	3	4	5	6	7	8	9	10
	Careless Mistakes	1	2	3	4	5	6	7	8	9	10
	Short Attention	1	2	3	4	5	6	7	8	9	10
	Forgetfulness	1	2	3	4	5	6	7	8	9	10

Date _____

DAILY PLANNER

Today's goals

Mood:

Priorities with Consequences

A⁺

Water Intake:

A⁺

Things to get done today:

_____
_____
_____
_____
_____
_____
_____
_____

Today's appointment:

TIME:	EVENT:

A⁺

For tomorrow:

_____
_____
_____
_____
_____

		1	2	3	4	5	6	7	8	9	10
IMPULSIVITY	Easily Frustrated	1	2	3	4	5	6	7	8	9	10
	Acting Without Thikining	1	2	3	4	5	6	7	8	9	10
	Interrupting Others	1	2	3	4	5	6	7	8	9	10
	Emotional Outbursts	1	2	3	4	5	6	7	8	9	10
HYPERACTIVITY	Difficulty Sleeping	1	2	3	4	5	6	7	8	9	10
	Constantly Moving	1	2	3	4	5	6	7	8	9	10
	Unable to Sit Still / Fidgeting	1	2	3	4	5	6	7	8	9	10
	Excessive Talking	1	2	3	4	5	6	7	8	9	10
INATTENTION	Easily Distracted	1	2	3	4	5	6	7	8	9	10
	Careless Mistakes	1	2	3	4	5	6	7	8	9	10
	Short Attention	1	2	3	4	5	6	7	8	9	10
	Forgetfulness	1	2	3	4	5	6	7	8	9	10

Date _____

DAILY PLANNER

Today's goals

Mood:

😄 🙂 😐 🙁 😞

Water Intake:

💧💧💧💧💧💧💧💧

Priorities with Consequences

A⁺

A⁺

Things to get done today:

_____
_____
_____
_____
_____
_____
_____
_____

Today's appointment:

TIME:	EVENT:

A⁺

For tomorrow:

_____
_____
_____
_____
_____

		1	2	3	4	5	6	7	8	9	10
IMPULSIVITY	Easily Frustrated	1	2	3	4	5	6	7	8	9	10
	Acting Without Thikining	1	2	3	4	5	6	7	8	9	10
	Interrupting Others	1	2	3	4	5	6	7	8	9	10
	Emotional Outbursts	1	2	3	4	5	6	7	8	9	10
HYPERACTIVITY	Difficulty Sleeping	1	2	3	4	5	6	7	8	9	10
	Constantly Moving	1	2	3	4	5	6	7	8	9	10
	Unable to Sit Still / Fidgeting	1	2	3	4	5	6	7	8	9	10
	Excessive Talking	1	2	3	4	5	6	7	8	9	10
INATTENTION	Easily Distracted	1	2	3	4	5	6	7	8	9	10
	Careless Mistakes	1	2	3	4	5	6	7	8	9	10
	Short Attention	1	2	3	4	5	6	7	8	9	10
	Forgetfulness	1	2	3	4	5	6	7	8	9	10

DAILY PLANNER

TODAY'S GOALS

MOOD:

WATER INTAKE:

PRIORITIES WITH CONSEQUENCES

A⁺

A⁺

THINGS TO GET DONE TODAY:

_____
_____
_____
_____
_____
_____
_____
_____
_____

TODAY'S APPOINTMENT:

A⁺

TIME:	EVENT:

FOR TOMORROW:

_____
_____
_____
_____
_____

		1	2	3	4	5	6	7	8	9	10
IMPULSIVITY	Easily Frustrated	1	2	3	4	5	6	7	8	9	10
	Acting Without Thikining	1	2	3	4	5	6	7	8	9	10
	Interrupting Others	1	2	3	4	5	6	7	8	9	10
	Emotional Outbursts	1	2	3	4	5	6	7	8	9	10
HYPERACTIVITY	Difficulty Sleeping	1	2	3	4	5	6	7	8	9	10
	Constantly Moving	1	2	3	4	5	6	7	8	9	10
	Unable to Sit Still / Fidgeting	1	2	3	4	5	6	7	8	9	10
	Excessive Talking	1	2	3	4	5	6	7	8	9	10
INATTENTION	Easily Distracted	1	2	3	4	5	6	7	8	9	10
	Careless Mistakes	1	2	3	4	5	6	7	8	9	10
	Short Attention	1	2	3	4	5	6	7	8	9	10
	Forgetfulness	1	2	3	4	5	6	7	8	9	10

Date _____

DAILY PLANNER

Today's goals

Mood:
😄 🙂 😐 🙁 😢

Water Intake:
💧💧💧💧💧💧💧

Priorities with Consequences

A⁺

A⁺

A⁺

Things to get done today:
_____
_____
_____
_____
_____
_____
_____
_____

Today's appointment:

TIME:	EVENT:

For tomorrow:
_____
_____
_____
_____
_____

		1	2	3	4	5	6	7	8	9	10
IMPULSIVITY	Easily Frustrated	1	2	3	4	5	6	7	8	9	10
	Acting Without Thikining	1	2	3	4	5	6	7	8	9	10
	Interrupting Others	1	2	3	4	5	6	7	8	9	10
	Emotional Outbursts	1	2	3	4	5	6	7	8	9	10
HYPERACTIVITY	Difficulty Sleeping	1	2	3	4	5	6	7	8	9	10
	Constantly Moving	1	2	3	4	5	6	7	8	9	10
	Unable to Sit Still / Fidgeting	1	2	3	4	5	6	7	8	9	10
	Excessive Talking	1	2	3	4	5	6	7	8	9	10
INATTENTION	Easily Distracted	1	2	3	4	5	6	7	8	9	10
	Careless Mistakes	1	2	3	4	5	6	7	8	9	10
	Short Attention	1	2	3	4	5	6	7	8	9	10
	Forgetfulness	1	2	3	4	5	6	7	8	9	10

DAILY PLANNER

TODAY'S GOALS

MOOD:

WATER INTAKE:

PRIORITIES WITH CONSEQUENCES

A⁺

A⁺

THINGS TO GET DONE TODAY:

TODAY'S APPOINTMENT:

A⁺

TIME: EVENT:

FOR TOMORROW:

		1	2	3	4	5	6	7	8	9	10
IMPULSIVITY	Easily Frustrated	1	2	3	4	5	6	7	8	9	10
	Acting Without Thikining	1	2	3	4	5	6	7	8	9	10
	Interrupting Others	1	2	3	4	5	6	7	8	9	10
	Emotional Outbursts	1	2	3	4	5	6	7	8	9	10
HYPERACTIVITY	Difficulty Sleeping	1	2	3	4	5	6	7	8	9	10
	Constantly Moving	1	2	3	4	5	6	7	8	9	10
	Unable to Sit Still / Fidgeting	1	2	3	4	5	6	7	8	9	10
	Excessive Talking	1	2	3	4	5	6	7	8	9	10
INATTENTION	Easily Distracted	1	2	3	4	5	6	7	8	9	10
	Careless Mistakes	1	2	3	4	5	6	7	8	9	10
	Short Attention	1	2	3	4	5	6	7	8	9	10
	Forgetfulness	1	2	3	4	5	6	7	8	9	10

MEDICATION
Tracker

	MEDICATION	DOSAGE	FREQUENCY	TAKEN
MONDAY				
TUESDAY				
WEDNESDAY				
THURSDAY				
FRIDAY				
SATURDAY				
SUNDAY				

NOTES

Nothing like ADHD and a good
fight to the death to make time fly.

—RICK RIORDAN

TO DO'S
Weekly

MUST DO!

_____

_____

_____

IMPORTANT

- _____
- _____
- _____
- _____
- _____
- _____
- _____
- _____
- _____
- _____

LESS IMPORTANT

- _____
- _____
- _____
- _____
- _____
- _____
- _____
- _____
- _____
- _____

NOTES

_____   _____
_____   _____
_____   _____
_____   _____

In the power of fixing the attention lies the
most precious of the intellectual habits.
– ROBERT HALL

HABIT TRACKER
Weekly

HÁBITS	MON	TUES	WED	THU	FRI	SAT	SUN
_____	○	○	○	○	○	○	○
_____	○	○	○	○	○	○	○
_____	○	○	○	○	○	○	○
_____	○	○	○	○	○	○	○
_____	○	○	○	○	○	○	○
_____	○	○	○	○	○	○	○
_____	○	○	○	○	○	○	○
_____	○	○	○	○	○	○	○
_____	○	○	○	○	○	○	○
_____	○	○	○	○	○	○	○
_____	○	○	○	○	○	○	○
_____	○	○	○	○	○	○	○
_____	○	○	○	○	○	○	○
_____	○	○	○	○	○	○	○

HOW DID I DO?

BRAIN DUMP

Though Organizer

MUST DO	SHOULD DO
COULD START	MUST DO

DAILY PLANNER

Today's goals

Mood:

Water Intake:

Priorities with Consequences

A

A

A

Things to get done today:

_____
_____
_____
_____
_____
_____
_____
_____
_____

Today's appointment:

TIME: EVENT:

_____   _____
_____   _____
_____   _____
_____   _____
_____   _____
_____   _____

For tomorrow:

_____
_____
_____
_____
_____

		1	2	3	4	5	6	7	8	9	10
IMPULSIVITY	Easily Frustrated	1	2	3	4	5	6	7	8	9	10
	Acting Without Thikining	1	2	3	4	5	6	7	8	9	10
	Interrupting Others	1	2	3	4	5	6	7	8	9	10
	Emotional Outbursts	1	2	3	4	5	6	7	8	9	10
HYPERACTIVITY	Difficulty Sleeping	1	2	3	4	5	6	7	8	9	10
	Constantly Moving	1	2	3	4	5	6	7	8	9	10
	Unable to Sit Still / Fidgeting	1	2	3	4	5	6	7	8	9	10
	Excessive Talking	1	2	3	4	5	6	7	8	9	10
INATTENTION	Easily Distracted	1	2	3	4	5	6	7	8	9	10
	Careless Mistakes	1	2	3	4	5	6	7	8	9	10
	Short Attention	1	2	3	4	5	6	7	8	9	10
	Forgetfulness	1	2	3	4	5	6	7	8	9	10

Date _____

DAILY PLANNER

Today's goals

Mood:

😊 🙂 😐 🙁 😢

Water Intake:

💧💧💧💧💧💧💧💧

Priorities with Consequences

A⁺

A⁺

A⁺

Things to get done today:

_____
_____
_____
_____
_____
_____
_____
_____
_____

Today's appointment:

TIME:	EVENT:

For tomorrow:

_____
_____
_____
_____
_____

		1	2	3	4	5	6	7	8	9	10
IMPULSIVITY	Easily Frustrated	1	2	3	4	5	6	7	8	9	10
	Acting Without Thikining	1	2	3	4	5	6	7	8	9	10
	Interrupting Others	1	2	3	4	5	6	7	8	9	10
	Emotional Outbursts	1	2	3	4	5	6	7	8	9	10
HYPERACTIVITY	Difficulty Sleeping	1	2	3	4	5	6	7	8	9	10
	Constantly Moving	1	2	3	4	5	6	7	8	9	10
	Unable to Sit Still / Fidgeting	1	2	3	4	5	6	7	8	9	10
	Excessive Talking	1	2	3	4	5	6	7	8	9	10
INATTENTION	Easily Distracted	1	2	3	4	5	6	7	8	9	10
	Careless Mistakes	1	2	3	4	5	6	7	8	9	10
	Short Attention	1	2	3	4	5	6	7	8	9	10
	Forgetfulness	1	2	3	4	5	6	7	8	9	10

DAILY PLANNER

🎯 TODAY'S GOALS

MOOD:

😊 🙂 😐 🙁 😢

WATER INTAKE:

💧 💧 💧 💧 💧 💧 💧 💧

PRIORITIES WITH CONSEQUENCES

A⁺

A⁺

THINGS TO GET DONE TODAY:

_____
_____
_____
_____
_____
_____
_____
_____

TODAY'S APPOINTMENT:

TIME:	EVENT:

A⁺

FOR TOMORROW:

_____
_____
_____
_____
_____

		1	2	3	4	5	6	7	8	9	10
IMPULSIVITY	Easily Frustrated	1	2	3	4	5	6	7	8	9	10
	Acting Without Thikining	1	2	3	4	5	6	7	8	9	10
	Interrupting Others	1	2	3	4	5	6	7	8	9	10
	Emotional Outbursts	1	2	3	4	5	6	7	8	9	10
HYPERACTIVITY	Difficulty Sleeping	1	2	3	4	5	6	7	8	9	10
	Constantly Moving	1	2	3	4	5	6	7	8	9	10
	Unable to Sit Still / Fidgeting	1	2	3	4	5	6	7	8	9	10
	Excessive Talking	1	2	3	4	5	6	7	8	9	10
INATTENTION	Easily Distracted	1	2	3	4	5	6	7	8	9	10
	Careless Mistakes	1	2	3	4	5	6	7	8	9	10
	Short Attention	1	2	3	4	5	6	7	8	9	10
	Forgetfulness	1	2	3	4	5	6	7	8	9	10

 *Date* _____

DAILY PLANNER

Today's goals

Mood:

Priorities with Consequences

A⁺

Water Intake:

A⁺

Things to get done today:

_____
_____
_____
_____
_____
_____
_____
_____

Today's appointment:

TIME: EVENT:

A⁺

For tomorrow:

_____
_____
_____
_____
_____

		1	2	3	4	5	6	7	8	9	10
IMPULSIVITY	Easily Frustrated	1	2	3	4	5	6	7	8	9	10
	Acting Without Thikining	1	2	3	4	5	6	7	8	9	10
	Interrupting Others	1	2	3	4	5	6	7	8	9	10
	Emotional Outbursts	1	2	3	4	5	6	7	8	9	10
HYPERACTIVITY	Difficulty Sleeping	1	2	3	4	5	6	7	8	9	10
	Constantly Moving	1	2	3	4	5	6	7	8	9	10
	Unable to Sit Still / Fidgeting	1	2	3	4	5	6	7	8	9	10
	Excessive Talking	1	2	3	4	5	6	7	8	9	10
INATTENTION	Easily Distracted	1	2	3	4	5	6	7	8	9	10
	Careless Mistakes	1	2	3	4	5	6	7	8	9	10
	Short Attention	1	2	3	4	5	6	7	8	9	10
	Forgetfulness	1	2	3	4	5	6	7	8	9	10

DAILY PLANNER

Today's goals

Mood:

Water Intake:

Priorities with Consequences

A⁺

A⁺

A⁺

Things to get done today:

_____
_____
_____
_____
_____
_____
_____
_____
_____
_____

Today's appointment:

TIME:	EVENT:

For tomorrow:

_____
_____
_____
_____
_____

		1	2	3	4	5	6	7	8	9	10
IMPULSIVITY	Easily Frustrated	1	2	3	4	5	6	7	8	9	10
	Acting Without Thikining	1	2	3	4	5	6	7	8	9	10
	Interrupting Others	1	2	3	4	5	6	7	8	9	10
	Emotional Outbursts	1	2	3	4	5	6	7	8	9	10
HYPERACTIVITY	Difficulty Sleeping	1	2	3	4	5	6	7	8	9	10
	Constantly Moving	1	2	3	4	5	6	7	8	9	10
	Unable to Sit Still / Fidgeting	1	2	3	4	5	6	7	8	9	10
	Excessive Talking	1	2	3	4	5	6	7	8	9	10
INATTENTION	Easily Distracted	1	2	3	4	5	6	7	8	9	10
	Careless Mistakes	1	2	3	4	5	6	7	8	9	10
	Short Attention	1	2	3	4	5	6	7	8	9	10
	Forgetfulness	1	2	3	4	5	6	7	8	9	10

Date _____

DAILY PLANNER

TODAY'S GOALS

MOOD:

PRIORITIES WITH CONSEQUENCES

A⁺

WATER INTAKE:

A⁺

THINGS TO GET DONE TODAY:

_____
_____
_____
_____
_____
_____
_____
_____

TODAY'S APPOINTMENT:

TIME:	EVENT:

A⁺

FOR TOMORROW:

_____
_____
_____
_____
_____

		1	2	3	4	5	6	7	8	9	10
IMPULSIVITY	Easily Frustrated	1	2	3	4	5	6	7	8	9	10
	Acting Without Thikining	1	2	3	4	5	6	7	8	9	10
	Interrupting Others	1	2	3	4	5	6	7	8	9	10
	Emotional Outbursts	1	2	3	4	5	6	7	8	9	10
HYPERACTIVITY	Difficulty Sleeping	1	2	3	4	5	6	7	8	9	10
	Constantly Moving	1	2	3	4	5	6	7	8	9	10
	Unable to Sit Still / Fidgeting	1	2	3	4	5	6	7	8	9	10
	Excessive Talking	1	2	3	4	5	6	7	8	9	10
INATTENTION	Easily Distracted	1	2	3	4	5	6	7	8	9	10
	Careless Mistakes	1	2	3	4	5	6	7	8	9	10
	Short Attention	1	2	3	4	5	6	7	8	9	10
	Forgetfulness	1	2	3	4	5	6	7	8	9	10

Date _____

DAILY PLANNER

Today's goals

Mood:

:) :) :| :(:(

Water Intake:

⬦ ⬦ ⬦ ⬦ ⬦ ⬦ ⬦

Priorities with Consequences

[A⁺]

[A⁺]

[A⁺]

Things to get done today:

_____
_____
_____
_____
_____
_____
_____
_____
_____
_____

Today's appointment:

TIME:	EVENT:

For tomorrow:

_____
_____
_____
_____
_____

		1	2	3	4	5	6	7	8	9	10
IMPULSIVITY	Easily Frustrated	1	2	3	4	5	6	7	8	9	10
	Acting Without Thikining	1	2	3	4	5	6	7	8	9	10
	Interrupting Others	1	2	3	4	5	6	7	8	9	10
	Emotional Outbursts	1	2	3	4	5	6	7	8	9	10
HYPERACTIVITY	Difficulty Sleeping	1	2	3	4	5	6	7	8	9	10
	Constantly Moving	1	2	3	4	5	6	7	8	9	10
	Unable to Sit Still / Fidgeting	1	2	3	4	5	6	7	8	9	10
	Excessive Talking	1	2	3	4	5	6	7	8	9	10
INATTENTION	Easily Distracted	1	2	3	4	5	6	7	8	9	10
	Careless Mistakes	1	2	3	4	5	6	7	8	9	10
	Short Attention	1	2	3	4	5	6	7	8	9	10
	Forgetfulness	1	2	3	4	5	6	7	8	9	10

MEDICATION
Tracker

	MEDICATION	DOSAGE	FREQUENCY	TAKEN
MONDAY				
TUESDAY				
WEDNESDAY				
THURSDAY				
FRIDAY				
SATURDAY				
SUNDAY				

NOTES

Nothing like ADHD and a good
fight to the death to make time fly.

—Rick Riordan

TO DO'S
Weekly

Must Do!

_____

_____

_____

Important

- _____
- _____
- _____
- _____
- _____
- _____
- _____
- _____
- _____
- _____
- _____

Less important

- _____
- _____
- _____
- _____
- _____
- _____
- _____
- _____
- _____
- _____
- _____

Notes

_____   _____

_____   _____

_____   _____

_____   _____

In the power of fixing the attention lies the
most precious of the intellectual habits.
– ROBERT HALL

HABIT TRACKER
Weekly

HÁBITS	MON	TUES	WED	THU	FRI	SAT	SUN
_____	○	○	○	○	○	○	○
_____	○	○	○	○	○	○	○
_____	○	○	○	○	○	○	○
_____	○	○	○	○	○	○	○
_____	○	○	○	○	○	○	○
_____	○	○	○	○	○	○	○
_____	○	○	○	○	○	○	○
_____	○	○	○	○	○	○	○
_____	○	○	○	○	○	○	○
_____	○	○	○	○	○	○	○
_____	○	○	○	○	○	○	○
_____	○	○	○	○	○	○	○
_____	○	○	○	○	○	○	○
_____	○	○	○	○	○	○	○

HOW DID I DO?

"I have more thoughts before breakfast
than most people have all day."
— UNKNOWN

BRAIN DUMP

Though Organizer

MUST DO	SHOULD DO
COULD START	**MUST DO**

Date _____

DAILY PLANNER

TODAY'S GOALS

MOOD:

PRIORITIES WITH CONSEQUENCES

WATER INTAKE:

THINGS TO GET DONE TODAY:

_____
_____
_____
_____
_____
_____
_____
_____

TODAY'S APPOINTMENT:

TIME: EVENT:

FOR TOMORROW:

_____
_____
_____
_____

		1	2	3	4	5	6	7	8	9	10
IMPULSIVITY	Easily Frustrated	1	2	3	4	5	6	7	8	9	10
	Acting Without Thikining	1	2	3	4	5	6	7	8	9	10
	Interrupting Others	1	2	3	4	5	6	7	8	9	10
	Emotional Outbursts	1	2	3	4	5	6	7	8	9	10
HYPERACTIVITY	Difficulty Sleeping	1	2	3	4	5	6	7	8	9	10
	Constantly Moving	1	2	3	4	5	6	7	8	9	10
	Unable to Sit Still / Fidgeting	1	2	3	4	5	6	7	8	9	10
	Excessive Talking	1	2	3	4	5	6	7	8	9	10
INATTENTION	Easily Distracted	1	2	3	4	5	6	7	8	9	10
	Careless Mistakes	1	2	3	4	5	6	7	8	9	10
	Short Attention	1	2	3	4	5	6	7	8	9	10
	Forgetfulness	1	2	3	4	5	6	7	8	9	10

Date _____

DAILY PLANNER

TODAY'S GOALS

MOOD:

😀 🙂 😐 🙁 😢

WATER INTAKE:

⬡ ⬡ ⬡ ⬡ ⬡ ⬡ ⬡

PRIORITIES WITH CONSEQUENCES

A⁺

A⁺

THINGS TO GET DONE TODAY:

_____
_____
_____
_____
_____
_____
_____
_____

TODAY'S APPOINTMENT:

TIME:	EVENT:

A⁺

FOR TOMORROW:

_____
_____
_____
_____
_____

		1	2	3	4	5	6	7	8	9	10
IMPULSIVITY	Easily Frustrated	1	2	3	4	5	6	7	8	9	10
	Acting Without Thikining	1	2	3	4	5	6	7	8	9	10
	Interrupting Others	1	2	3	4	5	6	7	8	9	10
	Emotional Outbursts	1	2	3	4	5	6	7	8	9	10
HYPERACTIVITY	Difficulty Sleeping	1	2	3	4	5	6	7	8	9	10
	Constantly Moving	1	2	3	4	5	6	7	8	9	10
	Unable to Sit Still / Fidgeting	1	2	3	4	5	6	7	8	9	10
	Excessive Talking	1	2	3	4	5	6	7	8	9	10
INATTENTION	Easily Distracted	1	2	3	4	5	6	7	8	9	10
	Careless Mistakes	1	2	3	4	5	6	7	8	9	10
	Short Attention	1	2	3	4	5	6	7	8	9	10
	Forgetfulness	1	2	3	4	5	6	7	8	9	10

DAILY PLANNER

TODAY'S GOALS

MOOD:

😊 🙂 😐 🙁 😢

WATER INTAKE:

PRIORITIES WITH CONSEQUENCES

A⁺

A⁺

THINGS TO GET DONE TODAY:

TODAY'S APPOINTMENT:

A⁺

TIME: EVENT:

FOR TOMORROW:

		1	2	3	4	5	6	7	8	9	10
IMPULSIVITY	Easily Frustrated	1	2	3	4	5	6	7	8	9	10
	Acting Without Thikining	1	2	3	4	5	6	7	8	9	10
	Interrupting Others	1	2	3	4	5	6	7	8	9	10
	Emotional Outbursts	1	2	3	4	5	6	7	8	9	10
HYPERACTIVITY	Difficulty Sleeping	1	2	3	4	5	6	7	8	9	10
	Constantly Moving	1	2	3	4	5	6	7	8	9	10
	Unable to Sit Still / Fidgeting	1	2	3	4	5	6	7	8	9	10
	Excessive Talking	1	2	3	4	5	6	7	8	9	10
INATTENTION	Easily Distracted	1	2	3	4	5	6	7	8	9	10
	Careless Mistakes	1	2	3	4	5	6	7	8	9	10
	Short Attention	1	2	3	4	5	6	7	8	9	10
	Forgetfulness	1	2	3	4	5	6	7	8	9	10

Date _____

DAILY PLANNER

Today's goals

Mood:

😊 🙂 😐 🙁 😣

Water Intake:

💧 💧 💧 💧 💧 💧 💧 💧

Priorities with Consequences

A⁺

A⁺

A⁺

Things to get done today:

_____
_____
_____
_____
_____
_____
_____

Today's appointment:

TIME:	EVENT:

For tomorrow:

_____
_____
_____
_____
_____

		1	2	3	4	5	6	7	8	9	10
IMPULSIVITY	Easily Frustrated	1	2	3	4	5	6	7	8	9	10
	Acting Without Thikining	1	2	3	4	5	6	7	8	9	10
	Interrupting Others	1	2	3	4	5	6	7	8	9	10
	Emotional Outbursts	1	2	3	4	5	6	7	8	9	10
HYPERACTIVITY	Difficulty Sleeping	1	2	3	4	5	6	7	8	9	10
	Constantly Moving	1	2	3	4	5	6	7	8	9	10
	Unable to Sit Still / Fidgeting	1	2	3	4	5	6	7	8	9	10
	Excessive Talking	1	2	3	4	5	6	7	8	9	10
INATTENTION	Easily Distracted	1	2	3	4	5	6	7	8	9	10
	Careless Mistakes	1	2	3	4	5	6	7	8	9	10
	Short Attention	1	2	3	4	5	6	7	8	9	10
	Forgetfulness	1	2	3	4	5	6	7	8	9	10

DAILY PLANNER

TODAY'S GOALS	MOOD:	PRIORITIES WITH CONSEQUENCES

MOOD:

😄 🙂 😐 🙁 😞

WATER INTAKE:

💧💧💧💧💧💧💧💧

THINGS TO GET DONE TODAY:	TODAY'S APPOINTMENT:	

TIME: EVENT:

FOR TOMORROW:

		1	2	3	4	5	6	7	8	9	10
IMPULSIVITY	Easily Frustrated	1	2	3	4	5	6	7	8	9	10
	Acting Without Thikining	1	2	3	4	5	6	7	8	9	10
	Interrupting Others	1	2	3	4	5	6	7	8	9	10
	Emotional Outbursts	1	2	3	4	5	6	7	8	9	10
HYPERACTIVITY	Difficulty Sleeping	1	2	3	4	5	6	7	8	9	10
	Constantly Moving	1	2	3	4	5	6	7	8	9	10
	Unable to Sit Still / Fidgeting	1	2	3	4	5	6	7	8	9	10
	Excessive Talking	1	2	3	4	5	6	7	8	9	10
INATTENTION	Easily Distracted	1	2	3	4	5	6	7	8	9	10
	Careless Mistakes	1	2	3	4	5	6	7	8	9	10
	Short Attention	1	2	3	4	5	6	7	8	9	10
	Forgetfulness	1	2	3	4	5	6	7	8	9	10

DAILY PLANNER

🎯 Today's Goals

Mood:

😄 🙂 😐 🙁 😢

Water Intake:

◇ ◇ ◇ ◇ ◇ ◇ ◇ ◇

Priorities with Consequences

A⁺

A⁺

Things to get done today:

_____
_____
_____
_____
_____
_____
_____

Today's Appointment:

TIME:	EVENT:

A⁺

For tomorrow:

_____
_____
_____
_____

		1	2	3	4	5	6	7	8	9	10
IMPULSIVITY	Easily Frustrated	1	2	3	4	5	6	7	8	9	10
	Acting Without Thikining	1	2	3	4	5	6	7	8	9	10
	Interrupting Others	1	2	3	4	5	6	7	8	9	10
	Emotional Outbursts	1	2	3	4	5	6	7	8	9	10
HYPERACTIVITY	Difficulty Sleeping	1	2	3	4	5	6	7	8	9	10
	Constantly Moving	1	2	3	4	5	6	7	8	9	10
	Unable to Sit Still / Fidgeting	1	2	3	4	5	6	7	8	9	10
	Excessive Talking	1	2	3	4	5	6	7	8	9	10
INATTENTION	Easily Distracted	1	2	3	4	5	6	7	8	9	10
	Careless Mistakes	1	2	3	4	5	6	7	8	9	10
	Short Attention	1	2	3	4	5	6	7	8	9	10
	Forgetfulness	1	2	3	4	5	6	7	8	9	10

Date _____

DAILY PLANNER

🎯 **TODAY'S GOALS**

MOOD:

😄 🙂 😐 🙁 😞

WATER INTAKE:

💧 💧 💧 💧 💧 💧 💧

PRIORITIES WITH CONSEQUENCES

[A⁺]

[A⁺]

[A⁺]

THINGS TO GET DONE TODAY:

_____
_____
_____
_____
_____
_____
_____
_____

TODAY'S APPOINTMENT:

TIME:	EVENT:

FOR TOMORROW:

_____
_____
_____
_____

		1	2	3	4	5	6	7	8	9	10
IMPULSIVITY	Easily Frustrated	1	2	3	4	5	6	7	8	9	10
	Acting Without Thikining	1	2	3	4	5	6	7	8	9	10
	Interrupting Others	1	2	3	4	5	6	7	8	9	10
	Emotional Outbursts	1	2	3	4	5	6	7	8	9	10
HYPERACTIVITY	Difficulty Sleeping	1	2	3	4	5	6	7	8	9	10
	Constantly Moving	1	2	3	4	5	6	7	8	9	10
	Unable to Sit Still / Fidgeting	1	2	3	4	5	6	7	8	9	10
	Excessive Talking	1	2	3	4	5	6	7	8	9	10
INATTENTION	Easily Distracted	1	2	3	4	5	6	7	8	9	10
	Careless Mistakes	1	2	3	4	5	6	7	8	9	10
	Short Attention	1	2	3	4	5	6	7	8	9	10
	Forgetfulness	1	2	3	4	5	6	7	8	9	10

MEDICATION
Tracker

	MEDICATION	DOSAGE	FREQUENCY	TAKEN
MONDAY				
TUESDAY				
WEDNESDAY				
THURSDAY				
FRIDAY				
SATURDAY				
SUNDAY				

NOTES

Nothing like ADHD and a good
fight to the death to make time fly.

—RICK RIORDAN

TO DO'S
Weekly

MUST DO!

_____
_____
_____

IMPORTANT

- _____
- _____
- _____
- _____
- _____
- _____
- _____
- _____
- _____
- _____

LESS IMPORTANT

- _____
- _____
- _____
- _____
- _____
- _____
- _____
- _____
- _____
- _____

NOTES

_____   _____
_____   _____
_____   _____
_____   _____

In the power of fixing the attention lies the
most precious of the intellectual habits.
— ROBERT HALL

HABIT TRACKER
Weekly

HÁBITS	MON	TUES	WED	THU	FRI	SAT	SUN
	○	○	○	○	○	○	○
	○	○	○	○	○	○	○
	○	○	○	○	○	○	○
	○	○	○	○	○	○	○
	○	○	○	○	○	○	○
	○	○	○	○	○	○	○
	○	○	○	○	○	○	○
	○	○	○	○	○	○	○
	○	○	○	○	○	○	○
	○	○	○	○	○	○	○
	○	○	○	○	○	○	○
	○	○	○	○	○	○	○
	○	○	○	○	○	○	○
	○	○	○	○	○	○	○

HOW DID I DO?

"I have more thoughts before breakfast
than most people have all day."
— UNKNOWN

BRAIN DUMP

Though Organizer

MUST DO	SHOULD DO
COULD START	MUST DO

Date _____

DAILY PLANNER

TODAY'S GOALS

MOOD:

😄 🙂 😐 🙁 ☹️

PRIORITIES WITH CONSEQUENCES

A⁺

WATER INTAKE:

◇ ◇ ◇ ◇ ◇ ◇ ◇

A⁺

THINGS TO GET DONE TODAY:

TODAY'S APPOINTMENT:

A⁺

_____
_____
_____
_____
_____
_____
_____
_____

TIME:	EVENT:

FOR TOMORROW:

_____
_____
_____
_____
_____

		1	2	3	4	5	6	7	8	9	10
IMPULSIVITY	Easily Frustrated	1	2	3	4	5	6	7	8	9	10
	Acting Without Thikining	1	2	3	4	5	6	7	8	9	10
	Interrupting Others	1	2	3	4	5	6	7	8	9	10
	Emotional Outbursts	1	2	3	4	5	6	7	8	9	10
HYPERACTIVITY	Difficulty Sleeping	1	2	3	4	5	6	7	8	9	10
	Constantly Moving	1	2	3	4	5	6	7	8	9	10
	Unable to Sit Still / Fidgeting	1	2	3	4	5	6	7	8	9	10
	Excessive Talking	1	2	3	4	5	6	7	8	9	10
INATTENTION	Easily Distracted	1	2	3	4	5	6	7	8	9	10
	Careless Mistakes	1	2	3	4	5	6	7	8	9	10
	Short Attention	1	2	3	4	5	6	7	8	9	10
	Forgetfulness	1	2	3	4	5	6	7	8	9	10

Date  _____

DAILY PLANNER

Today's goals

Mood:

😄 🙂 😐 🙁 😢

Water Intake:

Priorities with Consequences

A⁺

A⁺

A⁺

Things to get done today:

_____
_____
_____
_____
_____
_____
_____

Today's appointment:

TIME:	EVENT:

For tomorrow:

_____
_____
_____
_____
_____

		1	2	3	4	5	6	7	8	9	10
IMPULSIVITY	Easily Frustrated	1	2	3	4	5	6	7	8	9	10
	Acting Without Thikining	1	2	3	4	5	6	7	8	9	10
	Interrupting Others	1	2	3	4	5	6	7	8	9	10
	Emotional Outbursts	1	2	3	4	5	6	7	8	9	10
HYPERACTIVITY	Difficulty Sleeping	1	2	3	4	5	6	7	8	9	10
	Constantly Moving	1	2	3	4	5	6	7	8	9	10
	Unable to Sit Still / Fidgeting	1	2	3	4	5	6	7	8	9	10
	Excessive Talking	1	2	3	4	5	6	7	8	9	10
INATTENTION	Easily Distracted	1	2	3	4	5	6	7	8	9	10
	Careless Mistakes	1	2	3	4	5	6	7	8	9	10
	Short Attention	1	2	3	4	5	6	7	8	9	10
	Forgetfulness	1	2	3	4	5	6	7	8	9	10

DAILY PLANNER

TODAY'S GOALS

MOOD:

WATER INTAKE:

PRIORITIES WITH CONSEQUENCES

A⁺

A⁺

THINGS TO GET DONE TODAY:

_____
_____
_____
_____
_____
_____
_____

TODAY'S APPOINTMENT:

TIME:	EVENT:

A⁺

FOR TOMORROW:

_____
_____
_____
_____
_____

		1	2	3	4	5	6	7	8	9	10
IMPULSIVITY	Easily Frustrated	1	2	3	4	5	6	7	8	9	10
	Acting Without Thikining	1	2	3	4	5	6	7	8	9	10
	Interrupting Others	1	2	3	4	5	6	7	8	9	10
	Emotional Outbursts	1	2	3	4	5	6	7	8	9	10
HYPERACTIVITY	Difficulty Sleeping	1	2	3	4	5	6	7	8	9	10
	Constantly Moving	1	2	3	4	5	6	7	8	9	10
	Unable to Sit Still / Fidgeting	1	2	3	4	5	6	7	8	9	10
	Excessive Talking	1	2	3	4	5	6	7	8	9	10
INATTENTION	Easily Distracted	1	2	3	4	5	6	7	8	9	10
	Careless Mistakes	1	2	3	4	5	6	7	8	9	10
	Short Attention	1	2	3	4	5	6	7	8	9	10
	Forgetfulness	1	2	3	4	5	6	7	8	9	10

DAILY PLANNER

Today's goals

Mood:

Water Intake:

Priorities with Consequences

A⁺

A⁺

A⁺

Things to get done today:

_____
_____
_____
_____
_____
_____
_____
_____

Today's appointment:

TIME: EVENT:

For tomorrow:

_____
_____
_____
_____
_____

		1	2	3	4	5	6	7	8	9	10
IMPULSIVITY	Easily Frustrated	1	2	3	4	5	6	7	8	9	10
	Acting Without Thikining	1	2	3	4	5	6	7	8	9	10
	Interrupting Others	1	2	3	4	5	6	7	8	9	10
	Emotional Outbursts	1	2	3	4	5	6	7	8	9	10
HYPERACTIVITY	Difficulty Sleeping	1	2	3	4	5	6	7	8	9	10
	Constantly Moving	1	2	3	4	5	6	7	8	9	10
	Unable to Sit Still / Fidgeting	1	2	3	4	5	6	7	8	9	10
	Excessive Talking	1	2	3	4	5	6	7	8	9	10
INATTENTION	Easily Distracted	1	2	3	4	5	6	7	8	9	10
	Careless Mistakes	1	2	3	4	5	6	7	8	9	10
	Short Attention	1	2	3	4	5	6	7	8	9	10
	Forgetfulness	1	2	3	4	5	6	7	8	9	10

Date _____

DAILY PLANNER

Today's goals

Mood:

Water Intake:

Priorities with Consequences

Things to get done today:

_____
_____
_____
_____
_____
_____
_____
_____

Today's appointment:

TIME:	EVENT:

For tomorrow:

_____
_____
_____
_____
_____

		1	2	3	4	5	6	7	8	9	10
IMPULSIVITY	Easily Frustrated	1	2	3	4	5	6	7	8	9	10
	Acting Without Thikining	1	2	3	4	5	6	7	8	9	10
	Interrupting Others	1	2	3	4	5	6	7	8	9	10
	Emotional Outbursts	1	2	3	4	5	6	7	8	9	10
HYPERACTIVITY	Difficulty Sleeping	1	2	3	4	5	6	7	8	9	10
	Constantly Moving	1	2	3	4	5	6	7	8	9	10
	Unable to Sit Still / Fidgeting	1	2	3	4	5	6	7	8	9	10
	Excessive Talking	1	2	3	4	5	6	7	8	9	10
INATTENTION	Easily Distracted	1	2	3	4	5	6	7	8	9	10
	Careless Mistakes	1	2	3	4	5	6	7	8	9	10
	Short Attention	1	2	3	4	5	6	7	8	9	10
	Forgetfulness	1	2	3	4	5	6	7	8	9	10

Date _____

DAILY PLANNER

Today's Goals

Mood:

😊 🙂 😐 🙁 😢

Water Intake:

💧 💧 💧 💧 💧 💧 💧 💧

Priorities with Consequences

A⁺

A⁺

A⁺

Things to get done today:

_____
_____
_____
_____
_____
_____
_____
_____

Today's Appointment:

TIME:	EVENT:

For Tomorrow:

_____
_____
_____
_____
_____

		1	2	3	4	5	6	7	8	9	10
IMPULSIVITY	Easily Frustrated	1	2	3	4	5	6	7	8	9	10
	Acting Without Thikining	1	2	3	4	5	6	7	8	9	10
	Interrupting Others	1	2	3	4	5	6	7	8	9	10
	Emotional Outbursts	1	2	3	4	5	6	7	8	9	10
HYPERACTIVITY	Difficulty Sleeping	1	2	3	4	5	6	7	8	9	10
	Constantly Moving	1	2	3	4	5	6	7	8	9	10
	Unable to Sit Still / Fidgeting	1	2	3	4	5	6	7	8	9	10
	Excessive Talking	1	2	3	4	5	6	7	8	9	10
INATTENTION	Easily Distracted	1	2	3	4	5	6	7	8	9	10
	Careless Mistakes	1	2	3	4	5	6	7	8	9	10
	Short Attention	1	2	3	4	5	6	7	8	9	10
	Forgetfulness	1	2	3	4	5	6	7	8	9	10

Date _____

DAILY PLANNER

TODAY'S GOALS   MOOD: PRIORITIES WITH CONSEQUENCES

WATER INTAKE:

THINGS TO GET DONE TODAY: TODAY'S APPOINTMENT:

_____
_____
_____
_____
_____
_____
_____
_____
_____

TIME: EVENT:

FOR TOMORROW:

		1	2	3	4	5	6	7	8	9	10
IMPULSIVITY	Easily Frustrated	1	2	3	4	5	6	7	8	9	10
	Acting Without Thikining	1	2	3	4	5	6	7	8	9	10
	Interrupting Others	1	2	3	4	5	6	7	8	9	10
	Emotional Outbursts	1	2	3	4	5	6	7	8	9	10
HYPERACTIVITY	Difficulty Sleeping	1	2	3	4	5	6	7	8	9	10
	Constantly Moving	1	2	3	4	5	6	7	8	9	10
	Unable to Sit Still / Fidgeting	1	2	3	4	5	6	7	8	9	10
	Excessive Talking	1	2	3	4	5	6	7	8	9	10
INATTENTION	Easily Distracted	1	2	3	4	5	6	7	8	9	10
	Careless Mistakes	1	2	3	4	5	6	7	8	9	10
	Short Attention	1	2	3	4	5	6	7	8	9	10
	Forgetfulness	1	2	3	4	5	6	7	8	9	10

"It's like being a cat with 100 people with
laser pointers."
— JAMIE HYNDS

MEDICATION
Tracker

	MEDICATION	DOSAGE	FREQUENCY	TAKEN
MONDAY				
TUESDAY				
WEDNESDAY				
THURSDAY				
FRIDAY				
SATURDAY				
SUNDAY				

NOTES

Nothing like ADHD and a good
fight to the death to make time fly.

—Rick Riordan

TO DO'S
Weekly

Must Do!

_____
_____
_____

Important

- _____
- _____
- _____
- _____
- _____
- _____
- _____
- _____
- _____
- _____

Less important

- _____
- _____
- _____
- _____
- _____
- _____
- _____
- _____
- _____
- _____

Notes

_____   _____
_____   _____
_____   _____
_____   _____

In the power of fixing the attention lies the
most precious of the intellectual habits.
— ROBERT HALL

HABIT TRACKER
Weekly

HÁBITS	MON	TUES	WED	THU	FRI	SAT	SUN
	○	○	○	○	○	○	○
	○	○	○	○	○	○	○
	○	○	○	○	○	○	○
	○	○	○	○	○	○	○
	○	○	○	○	○	○	○
	○	○	○	○	○	○	○
	○	○	○	○	○	○	○
	○	○	○	○	○	○	○
	○	○	○	○	○	○	○
	○	○	○	○	○	○	○
	○	○	○	○	○	○	○
	○	○	○	○	○	○	○
	○	○	○	○	○	○	○
	○	○	○	○	○	○	○

HOW DID I DO?

"I have more thoughts before breakfast
than most people have all day."
— UNKNOWN

BRAIN DUMP
Though Organizer

MUST DO	SHOULD DO
COULD START	**MUST DO**

Date _____

DAILY PLANNER

TODAY'S GOALS

MOOD:

PRIORITIES WITH CONSEQUENCES

A⁺

WATER INTAKE:

A⁺

THINGS TO GET DONE TODAY:

TODAY'S APPOINTMENT:

A⁺

_____
_____
_____
_____
_____
_____
_____
_____

TIME: EVENT:

FOR TOMORROW:

_____
_____
_____
_____
_____

		1	2	3	4	5	6	7	8	9	10
IMPULSIVITY	Easily Frustrated	1	2	3	4	5	6	7	8	9	10
	Acting Without Thikining	1	2	3	4	5	6	7	8	9	10
	Interrupting Others	1	2	3	4	5	6	7	8	9	10
	Emotional Outbursts	1	2	3	4	5	6	7	8	9	10
HYPERACTIVITY	Difficulty Sleeping	1	2	3	4	5	6	7	8	9	10
	Constantly Moving	1	2	3	4	5	6	7	8	9	10
	Unable to Sit Still / Fidgeting	1	2	3	4	5	6	7	8	9	10
	Excessive Talking	1	2	3	4	5	6	7	8	9	10
INATTENTION	Easily Distracted	1	2	3	4	5	6	7	8	9	10
	Careless Mistakes	1	2	3	4	5	6	7	8	9	10
	Short Attention	1	2	3	4	5	6	7	8	9	10
	Forgetfulness	1	2	3	4	5	6	7	8	9	10

DAILY PLANNER

Today's goals

Mood:

Water Intake:

Priorities with Consequences

A⁺

A⁺

A⁺

Things to get done today:

_____
_____
_____
_____
_____
_____
_____
_____

Today's appointment:

TIME: EVENT:
_____
_____
_____
_____
_____

For tomorrow:

_____
_____
_____
_____
_____

		1	2	3	4	5	6	7	8	9	10
IMPULSIVITY	Easily Frustrated	1	2	3	4	5	6	7	8	9	10
	Acting Without Thikining	1	2	3	4	5	6	7	8	9	10
	Interrupting Others	1	2	3	4	5	6	7	8	9	10
	Emotional Outbursts	1	2	3	4	5	6	7	8	9	10
HYPERACTIVITY	Difficulty Sleeping	1	2	3	4	5	6	7	8	9	10
	Constantly Moving	1	2	3	4	5	6	7	8	9	10
	Unable to Sit Still / Fidgeting	1	2	3	4	5	6	7	8	9	10
	Excessive Talking	1	2	3	4	5	6	7	8	9	10
INATTENTION	Easily Distracted	1	2	3	4	5	6	7	8	9	10
	Careless Mistakes	1	2	3	4	5	6	7	8	9	10
	Short Attention	1	2	3	4	5	6	7	8	9	10
	Forgetfulness	1	2	3	4	5	6	7	8	9	10

DAILY PLANNER

Today's goals

Mood:

😊 🙂 😐 🙁 😢

Water Intake:

💧 💧 💧 💧 💧 💧 💧

Priorities with Consequences

A⁺

A⁺

A⁺

Things to get done today:

_____
_____
_____
_____
_____
_____
_____

Today's appointment:

TIME:	EVENT:

For tomorrow:

_____
_____
_____
_____
_____

		1	2	3	4	5	6	7	8	9	10
IMPULSIVITY	Easily Frustrated	1	2	3	4	5	6	7	8	9	10
	Acting Without Thikining	1	2	3	4	5	6	7	8	9	10
	Interrupting Others	1	2	3	4	5	6	7	8	9	10
	Emotional Outbursts	1	2	3	4	5	6	7	8	9	10
HYPERACTIVITY	Difficulty Sleeping	1	2	3	4	5	6	7	8	9	10
	Constantly Moving	1	2	3	4	5	6	7	8	9	10
	Unable to Sit Still / Fidgeting	1	2	3	4	5	6	7	8	9	10
	Excessive Talking	1	2	3	4	5	6	7	8	9	10
INATTENTION	Easily Distracted	1	2	3	4	5	6	7	8	9	10
	Careless Mistakes	1	2	3	4	5	6	7	8	9	10
	Short Attention	1	2	3	4	5	6	7	8	9	10
	Forgetfulness	1	2	3	4	5	6	7	8	9	10

Date _____

DAILY PLANNER

Today's goals

Mood:

Water Intake:

Priorities with Consequences

A+

A+

A+

Things to get done today:

_____
_____
_____
_____
_____
_____
_____
_____

Today's appointment:

TIME: EVENT:

For tomorrow:

_____
_____
_____
_____
_____

		1	2	3	4	5	6	7	8	9	10
IMPULSIVITY	Easily Frustrated	1	2	3	4	5	6	7	8	9	10
	Acting Without Thikining	1	2	3	4	5	6	7	8	9	10
	Interrupting Others	1	2	3	4	5	6	7	8	9	10
	Emotional Outbursts	1	2	3	4	5	6	7	8	9	10
HYPERACTIVITY	Difficulty Sleeping	1	2	3	4	5	6	7	8	9	10
	Constantly Moving	1	2	3	4	5	6	7	8	9	10
	Unable to Sit Still / Fidgeting	1	2	3	4	5	6	7	8	9	10
	Excessive Talking	1	2	3	4	5	6	7	8	9	10
INATTENTION	Easily Distracted	1	2	3	4	5	6	7	8	9	10
	Careless Mistakes	1	2	3	4	5	6	7	8	9	10
	Short Attention	1	2	3	4	5	6	7	8	9	10
	Forgetfulness	1	2	3	4	5	6	7	8	9	10

 Date _____

DAILY PLANNER

Today's Goals

Mood:

Priorities with Consequences

A⁺

Water Intake:

A⁺

Things to get done today:

Today's Appointment:

TIME: EVENT:

A⁺

For Tomorrow:

		1	2	3	4	5	6	7	8	9	10
IMPULSIVITY	Easily Frustrated	1	2	3	4	5	6	7	8	9	10
	Acting Without Thikining	1	2	3	4	5	6	7	8	9	10
	Interrupting Others	1	2	3	4	5	6	7	8	9	10
	Emotional Outbursts	1	2	3	4	5	6	7	8	9	10
HYPERACTIVITY	Difficulty Sleeping	1	2	3	4	5	6	7	8	9	10
	Constantly Moving	1	2	3	4	5	6	7	8	9	10
	Unable to Sit Still / Fidgeting	1	2	3	4	5	6	7	8	9	10
	Excessive Talking	1	2	3	4	5	6	7	8	9	10
INATTENTION	Easily Distracted	1	2	3	4	5	6	7	8	9	10
	Careless Mistakes	1	2	3	4	5	6	7	8	9	10
	Short Attention	1	2	3	4	5	6	7	8	9	10
	Forgetfulness	1	2	3	4	5	6	7	8	9	10

DAILY PLANNER

TODAY'S GOALS

MOOD:

WATER INTAKE:

PRIORITIES WITH CONSEQUENCES

A⁺

A⁺

THINGS TO GET DONE TODAY:

_____
_____
_____
_____
_____
_____
_____
_____
_____

TODAY'S APPOINTMENT:

TIME:	EVENT:

A⁺

FOR TOMORROW:

_____
_____
_____
_____
_____

		1	2	3	4	5	6	7	8	9	10
IMPULSIVITY	Easily Frustrated	1	2	3	4	5	6	7	8	9	10
	Acting Without Thikining	1	2	3	4	5	6	7	8	9	10
	Interrupting Others	1	2	3	4	5	6	7	8	9	10
	Emotional Outbursts	1	2	3	4	5	6	7	8	9	10
HYPERACTIVITY	Difficulty Sleeping	1	2	3	4	5	6	7	8	9	10
	Constantly Moving	1	2	3	4	5	6	7	8	9	10
	Unable to Sit Still / Fidgeting	1	2	3	4	5	6	7	8	9	10
	Excessive Talking	1	2	3	4	5	6	7	8	9	10
INATTENTION	Easily Distracted	1	2	3	4	5	6	7	8	9	10
	Careless Mistakes	1	2	3	4	5	6	7	8	9	10
	Short Attention	1	2	3	4	5	6	7	8	9	10
	Forgetfulness	1	2	3	4	5	6	7	8	9	10

Date _____

DAILY PLANNER

TODAY'S GOALS	MOOD:	PRIORITIES WITH CONSEQUENCES

MOOD:

😄 🙂 😐 🙁 😞

A⁺

WATER INTAKE:

💧💧💧💧💧💧💧

A⁺

THINGS TO GET DONE TODAY:

_____
_____
_____
_____
_____
_____
_____
_____
_____

TODAY'S APPOINTMENT:

A⁺

TIME:	EVENT:

FOR TOMORROW:

_____
_____
_____
_____
_____

		1	2	3	4	5	6	7	8	9	10
IMPULSIVITY	Easily Frustrated	1	2	3	4	5	6	7	8	9	10
	Acting Without Thikining	1	2	3	4	5	6	7	8	9	10
	Interrupting Others	1	2	3	4	5	6	7	8	9	10
	Emotional Outbursts	1	2	3	4	5	6	7	8	9	10
HYPERACTIVITY	Difficulty Sleeping	1	2	3	4	5	6	7	8	9	10
	Constantly Moving	1	2	3	4	5	6	7	8	9	10
	Unable to Sit Still / Fidgeting	1	2	3	4	5	6	7	8	9	10
	Excessive Talking	1	2	3	4	5	6	7	8	9	10
INATTENTION	Easily Distracted	1	2	3	4	5	6	7	8	9	10
	Careless Mistakes	1	2	3	4	5	6	7	8	9	10
	Short Attention	1	2	3	4	5	6	7	8	9	10
	Forgetfulness	1	2	3	4	5	6	7	8	9	10

MEDICATION
Tracker

	MEDICATION	DOSAGE	FREQUENCY	TAKEN
MONDAY				
TUESDAY				
WEDNESDAY				
THURSDAY				
FRIDAY				
SATURDAY				
SUNDAY				

NOTES

> Nothing like ADHD and a good
> fight to the death to make time fly.
>
> —RICK RIORDAN

TO DO'S
Weekly

MUST DO!

_____
_____
_____

IMPORTANT

- _____
- _____
- _____
- _____
- _____
- _____
- _____
- _____
- _____
- _____
- _____

LESS IMPORTANT

- _____
- _____
- _____
- _____
- _____
- _____
- _____
- _____
- _____
- _____
- _____

NOTES

_____   _____
_____   _____
_____   _____
_____   _____

In the power of fixing the attention lies the
most precious of the intellectual habits.
— ROBERT HALL

HABIT TRACKER
Weekly

HÁBITS	MON	TUES	WED	THU	FRI	SAT	SUN
_____	◯	◯	◯	◯	◯	◯	◯
_____	◯	◯	◯	◯	◯	◯	◯
_____	◯	◯	◯	◯	◯	◯	◯
_____	◯	◯	◯	◯	◯	◯	◯
_____	◯	◯	◯	◯	◯	◯	◯
_____	◯	◯	◯	◯	◯	◯	◯
_____	◯	◯	◯	◯	◯	◯	◯
_____	◯	◯	◯	◯	◯	◯	◯
_____	◯	◯	◯	◯	◯	◯	◯
_____	◯	◯	◯	◯	◯	◯	◯
_____	◯	◯	◯	◯	◯	◯	◯
_____	◯	◯	◯	◯	◯	◯	◯
_____	◯	◯	◯	◯	◯	◯	◯
_____	◯	◯	◯	◯	◯	◯	◯

HOW DID I DO?

*"I have more thoughts before breakfast
than most people have all day."*
— UNKNOWN

BRAIN DUMP
Though Organizer

MUST DO	SHOULD DO
COULD START	**MUST DO**

Date _____

DAILY PLANNER

Today's goals

Mood:

Priorities with Consequences

[A⁺]

Water Intake:

[A⁺]

Things to get done today:

Today's appointment:

[A⁺]

TIME: EVENT:

For tomorrow:

		1	2	3	4	5	6	7	8	9	10
IMPULSIVITY	Easily Frustrated	1	2	3	4	5	6	7	8	9	10
	Acting Without Thikining	1	2	3	4	5	6	7	8	9	10
	Interrupting Others	1	2	3	4	5	6	7	8	9	10
	Emotional Outbursts	1	2	3	4	5	6	7	8	9	10
HYPERACTIVITY	Difficulty Sleeping	1	2	3	4	5	6	7	8	9	10
	Constantly Moving	1	2	3	4	5	6	7	8	9	10
	Unable to Sit Still / Fidgeting	1	2	3	4	5	6	7	8	9	10
	Excessive Talking	1	2	3	4	5	6	7	8	9	10
INATTENTION	Easily Distracted	1	2	3	4	5	6	7	8	9	10
	Careless Mistakes	1	2	3	4	5	6	7	8	9	10
	Short Attention	1	2	3	4	5	6	7	8	9	10
	Forgetfulness	1	2	3	4	5	6	7	8	9	10

DAILY PLANNER

Today's Goals

Mood:

Water Intake:

Priorities with Consequences

A⁺

A⁺

A⁺

Things to get done today:

_____
_____
_____
_____
_____
_____
_____
_____

Today's Appointment:

TIME:	EVENT:

For tomorrow:

_____
_____
_____
_____

		1	2	3	4	5	6	7	8	9	10
IMPULSIVITY	Easily Frustrated	1	2	3	4	5	6	7	8	9	10
	Acting Without Thikining	1	2	3	4	5	6	7	8	9	10
	Interrupting Others	1	2	3	4	5	6	7	8	9	10
	Emotional Outbursts	1	2	3	4	5	6	7	8	9	10
HYPERACTIVITY	Difficulty Sleeping	1	2	3	4	5	6	7	8	9	10
	Constantly Moving	1	2	3	4	5	6	7	8	9	10
	Unable to Sit Still / Fidgeting	1	2	3	4	5	6	7	8	9	10
	Excessive Talking	1	2	3	4	5	6	7	8	9	10
INATTENTION	Easily Distracted	1	2	3	4	5	6	7	8	9	10
	Careless Mistakes	1	2	3	4	5	6	7	8	9	10
	Short Attention	1	2	3	4	5	6	7	8	9	10
	Forgetfulness	1	2	3	4	5	6	7	8	9	10

 *Date* _____

DAILY PLANNER

Today's goals

Mood:

😊 🙂 😐 ☹️ 😢

Priorities with Consequences

A⁺

Water Intake:

💧💧💧💧💧💧💧💧

A⁺

Things to get done today:

_____
_____
_____
_____
_____
_____
_____
_____

Today's appointment:

TIME:	EVENT:

A⁺

For tomorrow:

_____
_____
_____
_____
_____

		1	2	3	4	5	6	7	8	9	10
IMPULSIVITY	Easily Frustrated	1	2	3	4	5	6	7	8	9	10
	Acting Without Thikining	1	2	3	4	5	6	7	8	9	10
	Interrupting Others	1	2	3	4	5	6	7	8	9	10
	Emotional Outbursts	1	2	3	4	5	6	7	8	9	10
HYPERACTIVITY	Difficulty Sleeping	1	2	3	4	5	6	7	8	9	10
	Constantly Moving	1	2	3	4	5	6	7	8	9	10
	Unable to Sit Still / Fidgeting	1	2	3	4	5	6	7	8	9	10
	Excessive Talking	1	2	3	4	5	6	7	8	9	10
INATTENTION	Easily Distracted	1	2	3	4	5	6	7	8	9	10
	Careless Mistakes	1	2	3	4	5	6	7	8	9	10
	Short Attention	1	2	3	4	5	6	7	8	9	10
	Forgetfulness	1	2	3	4	5	6	7	8	9	10

DAILY PLANNER

Today's goals

Mood:

Water Intake:

Priorities with Consequences

A⁺

A⁺

A⁺

Things to get done today:

_____
_____
_____
_____
_____
_____
_____
_____

Today's appointment:

TIME: EVENT:

For tomorrow:

_____
_____
_____
_____

		1	2	3	4	5	6	7	8	9	10
IMPULSIVITY	Easily Frustrated	1	2	3	4	5	6	7	8	9	10
	Acting Without Thikining	1	2	3	4	5	6	7	8	9	10
	Interrupting Others	1	2	3	4	5	6	7	8	9	10
	Emotional Outbursts	1	2	3	4	5	6	7	8	9	10
HYPERACTIVITY	Difficulty Sleeping	1	2	3	4	5	6	7	8	9	10
	Constantly Moving	1	2	3	4	5	6	7	8	9	10
	Unable to Sit Still / Fidgeting	1	2	3	4	5	6	7	8	9	10
	Excessive Talking	1	2	3	4	5	6	7	8	9	10
INATTENTION	Easily Distracted	1	2	3	4	5	6	7	8	9	10
	Careless Mistakes	1	2	3	4	5	6	7	8	9	10
	Short Attention	1	2	3	4	5	6	7	8	9	10
	Forgetfulness	1	2	3	4	5	6	7	8	9	10

Date _____

DAILY PLANNER

Today's goals

Mood:

😄 🙂 😐 🙁 😞

Water Intake:

Priorities with Consequences

A⁺

A⁺

A⁺

Things to get done today:

_____
_____
_____
_____
_____
_____
_____
_____
_____

Today's appointment:

TIME:	EVENT:

For tomorrow:

_____
_____
_____
_____
_____

		1	2	3	4	5	6	7	8	9	10
IMPULSIVITY	Easily Frustrated	1	2	3	4	5	6	7	8	9	10
	Acting Without Thikining	1	2	3	4	5	6	7	8	9	10
	Interrupting Others	1	2	3	4	5	6	7	8	9	10
	Emotional Outbursts	1	2	3	4	5	6	7	8	9	10
HYPERACTIVITY	Difficulty Sleeping	1	2	3	4	5	6	7	8	9	10
	Constantly Moving	1	2	3	4	5	6	7	8	9	10
	Unable to Sit Still / Fidgeting	1	2	3	4	5	6	7	8	9	10
	Excessive Talking	1	2	3	4	5	6	7	8	9	10
INATTENTION	Easily Distracted	1	2	3	4	5	6	7	8	9	10
	Careless Mistakes	1	2	3	4	5	6	7	8	9	10
	Short Attention	1	2	3	4	5	6	7	8	9	10
	Forgetfulness	1	2	3	4	5	6	7	8	9	10

Date _____

DAILY PLANNER

TODAY'S GOALS

MOOD:

WATER INTAKE:

PRIORITIES WITH CONSEQUENCES

A⁺

A⁺

THINGS TO GET DONE TODAY:

_____
_____
_____
_____
_____
_____
_____

TODAY'S APPOINTMENT:

TIME:	EVENT:

A⁺

FOR TOMORROW:

_____
_____
_____
_____
_____

		1	2	3	4	5	6	7	8	9	10
IMPULSIVITY	Easily Frustrated	1	2	3	4	5	6	7	8	9	10
	Acting Without Thikining	1	2	3	4	5	6	7	8	9	10
	Interrupting Others	1	2	3	4	5	6	7	8	9	10
	Emotional Outbursts	1	2	3	4	5	6	7	8	9	10
HYPERACTIVITY	Difficulty Sleeping	1	2	3	4	5	6	7	8	9	10
	Constantly Moving	1	2	3	4	5	6	7	8	9	10
	Unable to Sit Still / Fidgeting	1	2	3	4	5	6	7	8	9	10
	Excessive Talking	1	2	3	4	5	6	7	8	9	10
INATTENTION	Easily Distracted	1	2	3	4	5	6	7	8	9	10
	Careless Mistakes	1	2	3	4	5	6	7	8	9	10
	Short Attention	1	2	3	4	5	6	7	8	9	10
	Forgetfulness	1	2	3	4	5	6	7	8	9	10

Date _____

DAILY PLANNER

Today's goals

Mood:

😄 🙂 😐 🙁 😞

Water Intake:

⬠⬠⬠⬠⬠⬠⬠⬠

Priorities with Consequences

A⁺

A⁺

A⁺

Things to get done today:

_____
_____
_____
_____
_____
_____
_____
_____
_____

Today's appointment:

TIME:	EVENT:

For tomorrow:

_____
_____
_____
_____
_____

		1	2	3	4	5	6	7	8	9	10
IMPULSIVITY	Easily Frustrated	1	2	3	4	5	6	7	8	9	10
	Acting Without Thikining	1	2	3	4	5	6	7	8	9	10
	Interrupting Others	1	2	3	4	5	6	7	8	9	10
	Emotional Outbursts	1	2	3	4	5	6	7	8	9	10
HYPERACTIVITY	Difficulty Sleeping	1	2	3	4	5	6	7	8	9	10
	Constantly Moving	1	2	3	4	5	6	7	8	9	10
	Unable to Sit Still / Fidgeting	1	2	3	4	5	6	7	8	9	10
	Excessive Talking	1	2	3	4	5	6	7	8	9	10
INATTENTION	Easily Distracted	1	2	3	4	5	6	7	8	9	10
	Careless Mistakes	1	2	3	4	5	6	7	8	9	10
	Short Attention	1	2	3	4	5	6	7	8	9	10
	Forgetfulness	1	2	3	4	5	6	7	8	9	10

MEDICATION
Tracker

	MEDICATION	DOSAGE	FREQUENCY	TAKEN
MONDAY				
TUESDAY				
WEDNESDAY				
THURSDAY				
FRIDAY				
SATURDAY				
SUNDAY				

NOTES

Nothing like ADHD and a good
fight to the death to make time fly.

—RICK RIORDAN

TO DO'S
Weekly

MUST DO!

_____
_____
_____

IMPORTANT

- _____
- _____
- _____
- _____
- _____
- _____
- _____
- _____
- _____
- _____

LESS IMPORTANT

- _____
- _____
- _____
- _____
- _____
- _____
- _____
- _____
- _____
- _____

NOTES

_____   _____
_____   _____
_____   _____

In the power of fixing the attention lies the
most precious of the intellectual habits.
– ROBERT HALL

HABIT TRACKER
Weekly

HÁBITS	MON	TUES	WED	THU	FRI	SAT	SUN
_____	○	○	○	○	○	○	○
_____	○	○	○	○	○	○	○
_____	○	○	○	○	○	○	○
_____	○	○	○	○	○	○	○
_____	○	○	○	○	○	○	○
_____	○	○	○	○	○	○	○
_____	○	○	○	○	○	○	○
_____	○	○	○	○	○	○	○
_____	○	○	○	○	○	○	○
_____	○	○	○	○	○	○	○
_____	○	○	○	○	○	○	○
_____	○	○	○	○	○	○	○
_____	○	○	○	○	○	○	○
_____	○	○	○	○	○	○	○

HOW DID I DO?

BRAIN DUMP

Though Organizer

MUST DO	SHOULD DO
COULD START	**MUST DO**

Date _____

DAILY PLANNER

Today's Goals

Mood:

Water Intake:

Priorities with Consequences

[A⁺]

[A⁺]

[A⁺]

Things to get done today:

_____
_____
_____
_____
_____
_____
_____
_____
_____

Today's appointment:

TIME:	EVENT:

For tomorrow:

_____
_____
_____
_____
_____

		1	2	3	4	5	6	7	8	9	10
IMPULSIVITY	Easily Frustrated	1	2	3	4	5	6	7	8	9	10
	Acting Without Thikining	1	2	3	4	5	6	7	8	9	10
	Interrupting Others	1	2	3	4	5	6	7	8	9	10
	Emotional Outbursts	1	2	3	4	5	6	7	8	9	10
HYPERACTIVITY	Difficulty Sleeping	1	2	3	4	5	6	7	8	9	10
	Constantly Moving	1	2	3	4	5	6	7	8	9	10
	Unable to Sit Still / Fidgeting	1	2	3	4	5	6	7	8	9	10
	Excessive Talking	1	2	3	4	5	6	7	8	9	10
INATTENTION	Easily Distracted	1	2	3	4	5	6	7	8	9	10
	Careless Mistakes	1	2	3	4	5	6	7	8	9	10
	Short Attention	1	2	3	4	5	6	7	8	9	10
	Forgetfulness	1	2	3	4	5	6	7	8	9	10

Date _____

DAILY PLANNER

Today's goals

Mood:

😄 🙂 😐 🙁 😢

Water Intake:

💧 💧 💧 💧 💧 💧 💧 💧

Priorities with Consequences

A⁺

A⁺

A⁺

Things to get done today:

_____
_____
_____
_____
_____
_____
_____
_____

Today's appointment:

TIME:	EVENT:

For tomorrow:

_____
_____
_____
_____
_____

		1	2	3	4	5	6	7	8	9	10
IMPULSIVITY	Easily Frustrated	1	2	3	4	5	6	7	8	9	10
	Acting Without Thikining	1	2	3	4	5	6	7	8	9	10
	Interrupting Others	1	2	3	4	5	6	7	8	9	10
	Emotional Outbursts	1	2	3	4	5	6	7	8	9	10
HYPERACTIVITY	Difficulty Sleeping	1	2	3	4	5	6	7	8	9	10
	Constantly Moving	1	2	3	4	5	6	7	8	9	10
	Unable to Sit Still / Fidgeting	1	2	3	4	5	6	7	8	9	10
	Excessive Talking	1	2	3	4	5	6	7	8	9	10
INATTENTION	Easily Distracted	1	2	3	4	5	6	7	8	9	10
	Careless Mistakes	1	2	3	4	5	6	7	8	9	10
	Short Attention	1	2	3	4	5	6	7	8	9	10
	Forgetfulness	1	2	3	4	5	6	7	8	9	10

DAILY PLANNER

TODAY'S GOALS

MOOD:

😊 🙂 😐 🙁 😟

WATER INTAKE:

💧💧💧💧💧💧💧

PRIORITIES WITH CONSEQUENCES

A⁺

A⁺

A⁺

THINGS TO GET DONE TODAY:

_____
_____
_____
_____
_____
_____
_____
_____
_____

TODAY'S APPOINTMENT:

TIME:	EVENT:

FOR TOMORROW:

_____
_____
_____
_____
_____

		1	2	3	4	5	6	7	8	9	10
IMPULSIVITY	Easily Frustrated	1	2	3	4	5	6	7	8	9	10
	Acting Without Thikining	1	2	3	4	5	6	7	8	9	10
	Interrupting Others	1	2	3	4	5	6	7	8	9	10
	Emotional Outbursts	1	2	3	4	5	6	7	8	9	10
HYPERACTIVITY	Difficulty Sleeping	1	2	3	4	5	6	7	8	9	10
	Constantly Moving	1	2	3	4	5	6	7	8	9	10
	Unable to Sit Still / Fidgeting	1	2	3	4	5	6	7	8	9	10
	Excessive Talking	1	2	3	4	5	6	7	8	9	10
INATTENTION	Easily Distracted	1	2	3	4	5	6	7	8	9	10
	Careless Mistakes	1	2	3	4	5	6	7	8	9	10
	Short Attention	1	2	3	4	5	6	7	8	9	10
	Forgetfulness	1	2	3	4	5	6	7	8	9	10

Date _____

DAILY PLANNER

Today's goals

Mood:
😄 🙂 😐 🙁 😣

Water Intake:
💧💧💧💧💧💧💧💧

Priorities with Consequences
A⁺

A⁺

A⁺

Things to get done today:
_____
_____
_____
_____
_____
_____
_____

Today's appointment:
TIME: EVENT:

For tomorrow:
_____
_____
_____
_____
_____

		1	2	3	4	5	6	7	8	9	10
IMPULSIVITY	Easily Frustrated	1	2	3	4	5	6	7	8	9	10
	Acting Without Thikining	1	2	3	4	5	6	7	8	9	10
	Interrupting Others	1	2	3	4	5	6	7	8	9	10
	Emotional Outbursts	1	2	3	4	5	6	7	8	9	10
HYPERACTIVITY	Difficulty Sleeping	1	2	3	4	5	6	7	8	9	10
	Constantly Moving	1	2	3	4	5	6	7	8	9	10
	Unable to Sit Still / Fidgeting	1	2	3	4	5	6	7	8	9	10
	Excessive Talking	1	2	3	4	5	6	7	8	9	10
INATTENTION	Easily Distracted	1	2	3	4	5	6	7	8	9	10
	Careless Mistakes	1	2	3	4	5	6	7	8	9	10
	Short Attention	1	2	3	4	5	6	7	8	9	10
	Forgetfulness	1	2	3	4	5	6	7	8	9	10

Date _____

DAILY PLANNER

Today's goals

Mood:
😀 🙂 😐 ☹️ 😣

Water Intake:
⬡ ⬡ ⬡ ⬡ ⬡ ⬡ ⬡

Priorities with Consequences

A⁺

A⁺

A⁺

Things to get done today:
_____
_____
_____
_____
_____
_____
_____
_____

Today's appointment:

TIME:	EVENT:

For tomorrow:
_____
_____
_____
_____
_____

		1	2	3	4	5	6	7	8	9	10
IMPULSIVITY	Easily Frustrated	1	2	3	4	5	6	7	8	9	10
	Acting Without Thikining	1	2	3	4	5	6	7	8	9	10
	Interrupting Others	1	2	3	4	5	6	7	8	9	10
	Emotional Outbursts	1	2	3	4	5	6	7	8	9	10
HYPERACTIVITY	Difficulty Sleeping	1	2	3	4	5	6	7	8	9	10
	Constantly Moving	1	2	3	4	5	6	7	8	9	10
	Unable to Sit Still / Fidgeting	1	2	3	4	5	6	7	8	9	10
	Excessive Talking	1	2	3	4	5	6	7	8	9	10
INATTENTION	Easily Distracted	1	2	3	4	5	6	7	8	9	10
	Careless Mistakes	1	2	3	4	5	6	7	8	9	10
	Short Attention	1	2	3	4	5	6	7	8	9	10
	Forgetfulness	1	2	3	4	5	6	7	8	9	10

Date _____

DAILY PLANNER

Today's goals

Mood:

Priorities with Consequences

A⁺

Water Intake:

A⁺

Things to get done today:

_____
_____
_____
_____
_____
_____
_____
_____

Today's appointment:

TIME: EVENT:

_____
_____
_____
_____
_____
_____

A⁺

For tomorrow:

_____
_____
_____
_____
_____

		1	2	3	4	5	6	7	8	9	10
IMPULSIVITY	Easily Frustrated	1	2	3	4	5	6	7	8	9	10
	Acting Without Thikining	1	2	3	4	5	6	7	8	9	10
	Interrupting Others	1	2	3	4	5	6	7	8	9	10
	Emotional Outbursts	1	2	3	4	5	6	7	8	9	10
HYPERACTIVITY	Difficulty Sleeping	1	2	3	4	5	6	7	8	9	10
	Constantly Moving	1	2	3	4	5	6	7	8	9	10
	Unable to Sit Still / Fidgeting	1	2	3	4	5	6	7	8	9	10
	Excessive Talking	1	2	3	4	5	6	7	8	9	10
INATTENTION	Easily Distracted	1	2	3	4	5	6	7	8	9	10
	Careless Mistakes	1	2	3	4	5	6	7	8	9	10
	Short Attention	1	2	3	4	5	6	7	8	9	10
	Forgetfulness	1	2	3	4	5	6	7	8	9	10

Date _____

DAILY PLANNER

Today's goals

Mood:

Priorities with Consequences

Water Intake:

A⁺

A⁺

Things to get done today:

Today's appointment:

A⁺

_____

TIME: EVENT:

_____

_____

For tomorrow:

_____

_____

_____

_____

_____

_____

_____

_____

_____

_____

		1	2	3	4	5	6	7	8	9	10
Impulsivity	Easily Frustrated	1	2	3	4	5	6	7	8	9	10
	Acting Without Thikining	1	2	3	4	5	6	7	8	9	10
	Interrupting Others	1	2	3	4	5	6	7	8	9	10
	Emotional Outbursts	1	2	3	4	5	6	7	8	9	10
Hyperactivity	Difficulty Sleeping	1	2	3	4	5	6	7	8	9	10
	Constantly Moving	1	2	3	4	5	6	7	8	9	10
	Unable to Sit Still / Fidgeting	1	2	3	4	5	6	7	8	9	10
	Excessive Talking	1	2	3	4	5	6	7	8	9	10
Inattention	Easily Distracted	1	2	3	4	5	6	7	8	9	10
	Careless Mistakes	1	2	3	4	5	6	7	8	9	10
	Short Attention	1	2	3	4	5	6	7	8	9	10
	Forgetfulness	1	2	3	4	5	6	7	8	9	10

MEDICATION

Tracker

	MEDICATION	DOSAGE	FREQUENCY	TAKEN
MONDAY				
TUESDAY				
WEDNESDAY				
THURSDAY				
FRIDAY				
SATURDAY				
SUNDAY				

NOTES

Made in the USA
Monee, IL
21 May 2022

96831077R00174